The Instrument Pilot's Library
• Volume Five •

IFR
Accidents

by
The Editors of *IFR* and *IFR Refresher*

Belvoir Publications, Inc.
Greenwich, Connecticut

ISBN: 1-879620-26-X

Printed and bound in the United States of America by Arcata Graphics, Fairfield, Pennsylvania.

Contents

Preface 5

Section One - Planning Ahead
• Avianca Flight 052 9
• Advance Warnings 17
• Routings and Refusals 23

Section Two - ATC's Role
• Controller Error 33
• Overriding the Controller 39
• Confusion on All Sides 45
• Confusing Instructons 55

Section Three - Equipment Failures
• Surviving Without Gyros 65
• Vacuum Failure: Nail in the Coffin 71
• Electrical Failure 77
• Reacting Appropriately 83

Section Four - Disorientation
• Mistaken Identity 91
• Confused and Disoriented 99
• The Drum DG Trap 105
• Disorientation in the Dark 111
• Doubly Lost 119

Section Five - Approach Accidents
• Two Accidents at Gainesville 129

- Deciding to Miss 143
- Preconceived Ideas 151
- Unfamiliar Approaches 159
- The Circling Approach 165

Section Six - Judgment: Pushing Limits
- Managing Risks 173
- Fighting Fatigue... 179
- Watching Your Fuel 195
- Weather Gambles... 205

Preface

When done properly, with a good level of caution and conservatism, instrument flying is not any more dangerous than flying VFR. Indeed, most accidents involving IFR conditions happen because VFR pilots fly into weather they're not trained to deal with.

Still, as the saying goes, accidents do happen. Given that we, as instrument-rated pilots, have (presumably) been trained to stay out of serious trouble, then why do IFR accidents occur?

Sometimes it's because a critical component fails, but that's more rare than one might imagine. Component failures, by themselves, cause few accidents.

Sometimes it's an unexpected, seemingly unavoidable weather phenomenon that causes an accident, like an embedded thunderstorm that was not forecast.

Most often, though, a given accident can be traced back to the pilot. Confusion, disorientation, failure to give up soon enough, inadequate preparation, or just plain poor judgment are all major causes of accidents.

On the premise that we can learn from the mistakes of others, in this volume of the *Instrument Pilot's Library* we'll discuss a variety of accidents with an eye towards how the pilot might have turned things around.

Naturally, hindsight is always perfect, and it's easy to say to ourselves after the fact, "Had *I* been there I would have done such-and-such differently. This accident would not have happened." Being in the cockpit is a different matter. Still, taking a close look at why accidents happen can provide valuable food for thought the next time you're faced with a potentially dicey situation.

One thing to keep in mind as you read this book is that few accidents are simple. Most have many causes, either building on one another or coming together at a critical moment. Each factor, by itself, may not have caused the accident: Taken together, they resulted in a tragedy. The key to avoiding such accidents (indeed, *any* accident) is to always be on the lookout for the warning signs and heed them before it's too late...even if the factor you're considering, by itself, should present no problem.

An instrument pilot should always be playing the "What if?" game. Is the forecast marginal? What if it's worse when I get there? What do I do then? What if I need to divert? What if I have an engine failure? What if I have to pick an alternate in a hurry (do I have the charts)?

This sort of thinking may seem paranoid, but as we'll see, if many of the pilots you're about to read about had paused the moment things began to look fishy and asked themselves if they were doing the right thing, they'd still be here to talk about it.

• Section One •

Planning Ahead

Avianca
Flight 052

T hough our first accident does not involve a general
aviation aircraft, it's a classic example of a flight
crew's failure to think ahead and thereby avert
disaster.

The case of Avianca 052 is most unusual, in that airliners virtually never
crash because they run out of fuel. There are so many safeguards built into the
regs that the possibility of a crew running the tanks dry is unheard of...that is,
until this accident took place.

As you read the account of the accident, try to put yourself in the pilot's
shoes. At what point would you have diverted?

Running Out of Options

It doesn't matter how many hours you have or the type of airplane you
fly, you're still vulnerable to making basic mistakes. For example, even
though the captain of Avianca 052 had 17,000 hours and flew a Boeing
707, he allowed himself to get painted into a corner until all his options
ran out.

January Flight

Avianca Airlines Flight 52 departed Medellin, Columbia for New York
JFK International with a crew of eight and 150 passengers. Their route
took them up the U.S. East Coast.

It was January and the weather that day in the eastern U.S. was
lousy. From a deep low over the Great Lakes, an occluded front
extended into northeastern New York, which bent south-southwest as
a cold front down through Pennsylvania and West Virginia. A station-

ary front paralleled the cold front to the east, from Virginia to New Jersey, southeastern New York and eastern Massachusetts. Low ceilings and rain extended from the Mid-Atlantic states into New England.

Fuel Requirements

The first critical event occurred during preflight planning. Avianca's dispatcher prepared the flight plan and weather data, and the airplane was fueled according to the following calculations:

Destination: 4 hours, 40 minutes
Holding: 30 minutes
Alternate: 30 minutes
Reserve: 28 minutes
Total: 6 hours, 8 minutes

There was a problem, however, with these calculations in that they were based on weather that was 9-10 hours old! We don't know why the crew didn't recognize their flight plan was based on old information. A check of current conditions before takeoff would have revealed JFK weather was near minimums and forecast to remain at or below minimums. Also, their alternate (Boston) was below alternate minimums and forecast to remain that way. Keep the fuel calculations in mind as you review the flight.

No Record of Updates

Avianca 52 departed Medellin at 1508 EST. There's no record of the crew contacting a flight service station, the company nor any contract service while en route to get updated weather and traffic information. Had the crew obtained an update, they would've known about the deteriorating weather and the extensive delays going into New York, thereby necessitating a change in plans.

Multiple Holds

As the flight progressed up the U.S. East Coast, it was placed in holding three times: the first was over Norfolk, VA for 19 minutes and the second was near Atlantic City, NJ for 29 minutes.

Avianca's fuel plan allocated only 30 minutes for holding. With the first hold lasting 19 minutes, their allocation was used 11 minutes into the second hold (four hours and 58 minutes after takeoff). This was another critical event for the flight, since this should have been the cutoff point for the crew to either continue to JFK or divert.

Instead, they waited another 15 minutes before asking ATC about delays, at which time they were told to expect another 30 minutes of delays in the New York area. The crew elected to continue toward JFK; a risky decision considering they were now eating into their alternate fuel.

The third hold came at 2018 (five hours and 10 minutes into the flight) at Camrn Intersection, 39 nm south of JFK. By conservative estimates, the B-707 had slightly less than one hour's fuel remaining.

The crew was given an expect further clearance (EFC) time of 2030 by New York Center, which was extended to 2039. After the second EFC lapsed, the first officer asked for a new EFC time. When the controller gave Avianca an EFC of 2105, the first officer responded:

Avianca: Well I think we need priority, we're passing (unintelligible).
Center: Avianca Zero-Five-Two-Heavy, roger, how long can you hold and what is your alternate?
Avianca 052: Stand by.

Aircraft were stacked up all over the New York area, leaving controllers in a quandary as to where to hold everyone. Another flight in holding asked if JFK was closed. The controller responded that several aircraft had missed the approach. The weather was hovering right at minimums. Avianca finally called back:

Avianca: We'll be able to hold about five minutes. That's all we can do.
Center: Avianca Zero-Five-Two-Heavy, roger, what is your alternate?
Avianca: Boston, but it is full of traffic I think.

The first officer's accent probably made communication difficult, which might have prompted the controller to ask again:

Center: Avianca Zero-Five-Two-Heavy, say again your alternate.
Avianca: It was Boston, but we can't do it now, we run out of fuel now.

Information Not Passed
The hand-off controller, who was assisting the Center radar controller handling Avianca, called New York Approach and said,

Center: Avianca Zero-Five-Two...can only do five more minutes in the hold. Think you'll be able to take him or I'll set him up for his alternate.

The good news was that Approach accepted Avianca. The bad news was that the hand-off controller didn't mention that Avianca had a fuel problem and couldn't make its alternate. (More about this later.)

The Center then cleared Avianca to the Kennedy Airport via heading 040, maintain 11,000, speed 180. Avianca departed holding at 2147 and contacted New York Approach as instructed. As a result of this clearance, the crew undoubtedly believed they were getting priority handling.

No Priority

The approach controller gave Avianca routine radar vectors in sequence with other traffic for the ILS Runway 22L. At approximately 2055 EST, the controller told Avianca to make a 360-degree turn for spacing behind traffic. It should have been clear to the crew by now they weren't getting priority handling.

The JFK weather was: ceiling indefinite 200 feet obscured, visibility one-quarter mile in light drizzle and fog, wind 180 at 22 gusting 28, Runway 4R visual range 1800 variable 2200 feet. Avianca was a Category D airplane, so the visibility was varying slightly above and below minimums. As if this wasn't bad enough, Approach told Avianca of a pilot report of wind shear on the approach, An increase of 10 knots at 1500 feet and then an increase of 10 knots at 500 feet.

During the next seven minutes, Avianca got several heading changes and further descent clearances to 3000 feet and finally to 2000 feet. Finally, the crew discussed whether they were getting expeditious handling. The captain's comprehension of English wasn't good, so he deferred to the second officer who said, "They are giving us priority."

At 2115, Avianca was approximately 15 miles from the outer marker when it was cleared for the approach. Kennedy Tower told the crew they were number three to land.

The approach was not a smooth one. The aircraft went from the lower limit of the glideslope to well above the glideslope. The captain remarked, "This is the wind shear."

The aircraft then sank so dangerously low that the ground proximity warning system (GPWS) announced, *Pull up!* four separate times. There were other factors contributing to this botched approach which we'll discuss shortly.

The crew never saw the runway environment and executed a missed approach. As the tower issued missed approach instructions, the captain said to the first officer, "Tell them we are in emergency."

Too Little, Too Late

Avianca: We're running out of fuel sir.

Approach: Avianca Zero-Five-Two-Heavy, I'm going to bring you about 15 miles northeast and then turn you back on for the approach. Is that fine with you and your fuel?
Avianca: I guess so, thank you very much.

This was a weak response given their desperate situation and the need for as close a turn back in as possible. By the time Avianca was 15 miles outside the marker for another approach, two engines had flamed out. Six hours and 26 minutes after takeoff, Avianca 52 crashed on a hillside in a residential area. 73 people died, including the crew. There was no fire. Only a small amount of residual fuel was found in the wreckage.

The crash site was just past Long Island's north shore. Had the airplane gone down a few seconds before, it would have landed in the water. Amazingly, it just missed plowing over a house.

Aftermath

You've probably guessed that the ensuing investigation by NTSB focused on the planning for the flight, the crew's performance during the flight and their handling by ATC.

As we mentioned earlier, investigators couldn't figure out why the crew didn't recognize the 10-hour old weather in their flight plan. With more current information, it's reasonable to assume they would've insisted on a different fuel plan and selected a suitable alternate. There were airports behind the front that would have been good alternates.

This flight departed with a severe handicap, made worse by the lack of in-flight updating. On a day when the weather stayed close to minimums, it's difficult to believe a professional crew waited so long to inquire about conditions ahead. In all fairness, we only have the last 40 minutes of the crew's cockpit conversation just before the accident, so we don't know what they discussed about weather and traffic prior to that time. We do know they asked ATC about Boston and further delays during the second hold.

Misunderstood Clearance?

The first indication to ATC of Avianca's fuel situation wasn't until the flight had been in holds totaling one hour and ten minutes. NTSB conjectured that the reason for this could have been a misunderstanding by the crew of the EFC times issued by ATC. The crew might have believed that the EFCs in the third hold (39 nm south of JFK) were times in which they would depart holding and begin the approach.

There's a big difference between an expect further clearance time and an expect approach clearance time. An EFC means you can expect either to be cleared for further holding or to another fix, but you shouldn't assume you'll be cleared for an approach after the EFC, unless ATC indicates otherwise.

It wasn't until ATC issued the third EFC that the crew asked for priority handling, but by this time, their holding and reserve fuel was gone and they were using precious fuel needed to go to their alternate. After telling ATC they couldn't make their alternate, Avianca flew for 47 minutes before crashing. 47 minutes was enough time to make something happen had they been more insistent.

When the flight left the third hold and was vectored with other traffic, including a three-sixty for spacing, the crew should have said the E word: EMERGENCY. The closest they ever came to declaring an emergency was during the missed approach when the first officer said, "We're running out of fuel."

Communications Breakdown

You'll recall that the Center hand-off controller didn't tell New York Approach about Avianca's fuel situation. During the investigation, the hand-off controller said he never heard Avianca's last remark about their alternate and fuel situation. As a result, the hand-off controller told New York Approach that Avianca could only hold an additional five minutes or it would have to divert.

The Center controller handed the flight over to Approach, believing he had accommodated Avianca's request for priority. Meanwhile, the crew believed they had communicated their critical fuel situation. You're probably thinking that if the controllers had asked further about the crew's fuel comment, the situation might have been clarified. Apparently, it didn't register with the controllers that the flight could have been within minutes of fuel starvation. (Remember that airliners *never* run out of fuel.) NTSB concluded that the flight was properly handled by ATC in light of the information supplied by the crew.

The Approach

The radar data depicts an unstabilized approach. Several significant factors contributed to this.

New York Approach told Avianca of wind shear reported by other flights during the approach. After reviewing ATC radar data, investigators found that the winds were generally aligned with the runway, but found that airplanes were flying into a decreasing headwind shear on the ILS. The wind speed was 60 knots or greater at 1000 feet, 50 knots at 500 feet and 20 knots at the surface.

These conditions require you to constantly adjust pitch and power while descending on the glideslope to compensate for the decreasing headwind. In this situation, groundspeed increases as the headwind decreases, requiring you to increase your descent rate to stay on the glideslope.

Unfortunately, the Avianca captain configured the airplane for a light or no headwind condition when he flew the glideslope. This resulted in a descent rate that was too steep, given the 60-plus knot winds at glideslope intercept, and the airplane immediately descended below the glideslope. The data shows constant chasing of the glideslope and a failure to stabilize the approach. Other airplanes of similar weight and speed to Avianca were completing this approach successfully.

Fatigue a Factor?

As if this wasn't bad enough, the autopilot in this airplane had recurring problems which included the altitude hold function and the ability to fly a coupled approach. Investigators believed that the airplane might have been hand-flown the entire flight and the ILS was flown without the aid of the autopilot or flight director.

From the time Avianca was on the final vector to the localizer until the missed approach, there were nine instances where the captain asked the first officer to repeat instructions or confirm the airplane's configuration. NTSB believed this problem and the unstabilized approach were signs that the captain was affected by fatigue and adverse stress.

Implications

You can't make an informed decision about your flight without the most current information. We've said many times that FAR 91.3 squarely places the responsibility for the safety of every flight on the pilot in command. Although many people get involved and influence your decisions, the ultimate responsibility can't be shared with anyone.

Flying into an area of widespread IFR conditions demands that you stay informed so you can realistically assess whether the flight can be completed as planned or whether you'll have to revert to Plan B.

Never paint yourself into a corner, nor let someone else lead you into a situation where you have few options to complete the flight safely. If you do get backed into a corner, the FARs give you all the necessary authority to declare an emergency and demand assistance from ATC.

The Avianca crew couldn't get ATC to understand their predicament, which was compounded by the controllers' distractions of heavy traffic due to poor weather. If the crew had made a more specific statement, such as, "We have less than one hour's fuel remaining and need an approach as soon as possible," the controller would have gotten the message. Clearly, the crew didn't understand that saying the word emergency was necessary to trigger all possible assistance.

Many critics argued that the controllers should have been more inquisitive when Avianca mentioned fuel problems, but the controllers handled the flight based on their understanding of the problem. The crew should have been more assertive as the fuel supply dwindled.

Finally, if you're ever in a situation where you must make an approach on the first try and a missed approach isn't an option, use all available resources to complete the approach successfully. If there's another pilot aboard, have that person monitor the approach and help you maintain a stabilized procedure. Tell ATC you have only one shot at making it and ask for all available assistance.

Advance Warnings

You may get through your entire IFR lifetime without once looking catastrophe in the eye. That's especially true if your instrument flying isn't accompanied by any urgency and cancellation and/or diversion isn't subject to anyone's review.

Despite a professional pilot's need to get an airplane to the appointed place on time—and sometimes with a great deal of urgency involved—there's always a personal review that should take place, that is, Are the conditions I'm facing on this flight worth the risk?

Since the pilot in command is charged with complete responsibility for the safety of each flight, all potentially limiting factors must be accounted for before departing. Sometimes, it's more sensible to stay on the ground, even if it inconveniences someone else.

If you've ever been in one of those binds where you need to get somewhere, the weather is bad and you know you shouldn't go, but you succumbed to the urgency and somehow squeaked through, you know that there were warning flags that if heeded would have saved a lot of stress and strain. We'll discuss these warning signs throughout the book. In this chapter, see if you can pick them out.

Is This Trip Really Necessary?

At 8:15 a.m. on January 31, the Teterboro, New Jersey Flight Service Station telephone was answered by a preflight briefer:

Pilot: Good morning, I'd like to check some weather around the Pittsburgh area. We're going into Latrobe [45 miles southeast of Pittsburgh), looking for an alternate. Maybe you can give me Latrobe weather currently also.

FSS: Okay, Latrobe now reporting 2500 overcast, visibility five miles in light rain and light freezing rain, temperature 36, dew point missing, wind 190 at 6, altimeter 2983. You had a briefing before this, right?

Pilot: Yeah, we had a complete briefing earlier, just looking for an alternate now. What's the Latrobe forecast?

FSS: Well, they don't give a terminal. But Pittsburgh, Allegheny County Airport, let's see, they're saying until 1600 Greenwich, 2500 overcast, four miles in freezing rain, ice pellets and snow, then 1100 overcast, three miles in light rain. Occasional 500 overcast, a mile and a half in light rain until 2200 Zulu.

With the knowledge that the pilot needed an airport with a forecast of at least 600 and 2, the briefer continued looking for potential alternates.

FSS: Let's see, for Columbus [Ohio], they would be no good for anything. They only have 400 and three-quarters. Philipsburg [PA] is no good, they only have 200 and a half. Harrisburg [PA], 200 and a half; Parkersburg, West Virginia 500 and a half. Let me check some more.

The bad weather apparently extended far afield that morning, because the next question from the briefer concerned the airplane's range after he said, "There's nothing for a legal alternate in Pennsylvania, West Virginia, Ohio, southern Michigan, western New York. This is ridiculous, everybody's going to be down under 400 and a half."

The pilot of the Cessna 414 consulted with his co-pilot and came up with a range of about four hours.

FSS: All right, just to have some kind of alternate, you may have to use something back towards this area. In fact, we're just starting to get some snow out the window now. But let's see, we've got 800 and two up until 1800 Greenwich in the local area. You'll have to use an alternate generally back in northern New Jersey unless we can find something a little bit closer, eastern Pennsylvania. We have to work our way backwards.

The transcript of the recorded conversation reveals that the briefer talked to himself for about 30 seconds while he perused the weather information. He finally said:

FSS: I would say the only place to go is east, so you have to use the metropolitan [New York] area I guess to find a legal alternate. There's nothing for Pennsylvania, New York, Ohio, Virginia, west Virginia, Indiana, Michigan. Nothing going to the Midwest.

Pilot: Our arrival time is about 1500Z, and ah, didn't you say Pittsburgh was 1100?

FSS: Let's see, yeah 1100 overcast and three in light rain, occasional 500 overcast, a mile and a half in light rain. So you can use that 500 and a mile and a half?

Pilot: No, that's not enough. I guess we'll have to come back here. Okay, how about throwing that in on a flight plan for N1994G, departing Teterboro at 1300Z.

The briefing ended at 8:17 a.m. and the C-414 was flown to Latrobe without incident. At 12:06 p.m., the airplane departed for Coatesville, Pennsylvania. On board was the captain (an ATP, current and qualified for FAR 135, although this was a FAR 91 corporate flight) and his co-pilot (a commercial pilot with 800- plus hours, but only 32 hours multi-engine). The captain had 49 hours in this airplane.

The Coatesville Airport has an ILS and a VOR approach. No weather reporting was available, but when N94G got the weather at Wilmington, Delaware (22 miles south), there was no doubt which procedure to use.

N94G: Philadelphia, Cessna One-Nine-Nine-Four-Golf descending to 6000.

ATC: Cessna Nine-Four-Golf, Philadelphia Approach, ident. Descend and maintain 5000.

N94G: Roger, Nine-Four-Golf, down to 5000.

ATC: Cessna Nine-Four-Golf, Greater Wilmington weather ATIS information Sierra. They're reporting indefinite 100, sky obscured, visibility is one mile in snow and fog. The surface wind is 110 at 6, altimeter 3003.

N94G: Roger, got the wind and altimeter. What was the rest of the weather?

ATC: Okay, the rest of the weather is indefinite ceiling 100, sky obscured, the visibility is one mile with light snow and fog. You can expect the ILS Runway 29 approach, vector to the final approach course. You can fly heading now of 120, maintain 5000.

The pilot of 94G then inquired if anyone else had made the approach at Coatesville and was told that there was another aircraft (coincidentally, another C-414) "...maybe about a half-hour ago, however, within the last 10 minutes I haven't had any."

N94G was cleared to 3000 and asked to cancel IFR with approach control or by telephone after landing. At 1:00 pm, N94G was turned southbound to intercept the localizer.

ATC: Cessna Nine-Four-Golf, you are five miles from Moses. Turn right heading 260, descend and maintain 2400 until you're established on the localizer. Cleared for ILS Runway 29 approach.
N94G: Right to 260 and cleared for the ILS. What was that altitude until established?
ATC: Descend and maintain 2400.
N94G: Roger, 2400.

One minute and forty-five seconds later, the controller observed N94G at the outer marker. He told the pilot of his position, terminated radar service and approved a change to the advisory frequency, "If you're able, report back on this frequency and advise canceling your IFR."

The pilot acknowledged and the next significant transmission was six and a half minutes later. The controller, concerned that he had not heard from N94G, broadcast in the blind:

ATC: Twin Cessna One-Nine-Nine-Golf, Philadelphia Approach.

There was no answer, because N94G was upside down, on fire and totally destroyed in the back yard of a residence one mile west of the airport. An otherwise routine ILS approach had turned completely sour.

Plenty of Witnesses

A lineman at the airport saw the twin through breaks in the overcast and noticed that the airplane was westbound with the landing gear extended. The Cessna quickly disappeared in the clouds and fog.

Another witness, standing in a parking lot off the departure end of the runway, saw the airplane coming toward him flying low, 80 to 100 feet high and rolling from left to right, slowly rising. This witness described the airplane as out of control. The Cessna continued to travel away from him until it turned almost completely perpendicular to the ground and descended.

Witnesses much closer to the crash site reported similar behavior before the crash, with complete agreement that the airplane had rolled into a near-vertical bank just before hitting the ground.

The pilot may have come close to pulling it off, because the twin hit the ground in a near-level attitude. Unfortunately, it slid directly into an above-ground swimming pool that contained a 12-inch thick disc of ice, enough to up-end the airplane and tear it apart. The pool also prevented the Cessna from continuing into the house, where a family was gathered for lunch.

The pilot of the other Cessna 414 that made the approach 30 minutes earlier was located. He said that he made two attempts, but couldn't land because the visibility was poor. On the first try, he saw nothing at DH. On the second approach, he saw the ground but no runway, so he executed the missed approach and flew to Philadelphia, where he landed without incident.

No Apparent Malfunctions

The wreckage was scattered along a distance of 250 feet from the swimming pool back to the initial impact point. The fuselage was inverted, the left propeller was separated from its engine, the landing gear was up and wing flaps were extended 30 degrees. Neither prop was feathered. A thorough investigation of the airplane's components and structures didn't reveal any evidence of malfunction.

Postmortem examination of the pilots didn't show any conditions that would have affected their abilities to operate the airplane.

The National Transportation Safety Board concluded that the accident was caused by an improper IFR procedure, followed by a failure to maintain airspeed and permit a stall and inadequate airplane handling by the pilot.

The eyewitness accounts suggest that the pilot was attempting a circling maneuver and lost control in a tight, low-altitude turn. Something drove the pilot to press on in the face of pretty serious IFR conditions. Was this trip really necessary?

The ILS approach at Coatesville isn't quite standard, in that DH is 300 feet and the visibility minimum is one mile. But given those minimums, if the runway isn't in sight at DH, there's precious little advantage in attempting a circle-to-land maneuver (to say nothing of the obvious illegality).Even if the pilot had decided to fly the length of the runway at DH in a low-visibility situation (still not a legal or proper procedure), he would have been faced with making a short-radius turn at the end if he had tried to land the other way.

When nothing happens visually at DH, you should feel free to come back and try again. But the outcome of pressing-on below DH or attempting a circle-to-land maneuver at that altitude is really asking for trouble.

Warnings Aplenty

How many times did your hazard alarm go off as you read this report? There were a number of them, and we hope that you'll remember and recognize them when similar circumstances show up as you go about your IFR business.

Routings and Refusals

Often, good IFR planning involves more than just weather considerations. Because of the seemingly twisted nature of ATC in certain parts of the country, an IFR pilot must often take into account the reroutings and amendments that ATC is bound to issue.

ATC in crowded parts of the country like the Northeast is like a force of nature. You can't beat it, you just have to learn to live with it. Just as you'll get wet if you walk out in the rain, if you make an IFR flight in the Northeast you'll get rerouted (well, not always, but it sure seems that way).

In this accident, the pilot planned for proper reserves, accounting for the forecast weather. But he didn't count on the inevitable reroute.

Planning for Diversions

"I have an amendment to your clearance, advise when ready to copy." These words from a controller are de rigeur when you're flying low-altitude IFR, especially in the super-busy Northeast Corridor (Washington, Philadelphia, New York, Boston). Some operators who fly the Corridor on a regular basis study the flow patterns and figure out ways to file so they don't wind up with routing amendments, but the average pilot will run afoul of this inconvenience sooner or later.

And it should be considered nothing more, nothing less than just that—an inconvenience. The rub comes in the form of an inevitable increase in flying time and that means more fuel burned. If nothing else, a pilot planning an instrument operation in the Corridor (as well as the other busy U.S. terminals) should expect to be rerouted somewhere along the line and always be prepared with extra fuel to accommodate it.

Here's an analytical look at an accident that probably would have happened anyway, but an amended clearance complicated things in terms of where the airplane came to rest. The crash locale might have made a world of difference in the outcome.

Routine, No Sweat

The trip began in New Haven, CT on a September morning. It was a dual-purpose flight: the pilot, a young CFI aspiring to an airline job could add the hours to his logbook, while his passenger could accomplish business in Biddeford, ME and get back to New Haven the same day.

The airplane was a Piper Archer operated on a lease-back arrangement and rented for the occasion from the FBO where the pilot worked.

Weather played a minor part in this episode. The NTSB reported only the conditions that existed near the accident site: Clouds were in the area. The pilot reported that he broke out of the clouds at 1600 feet. Islip Airport was reporting 1300 broken with 3000 feet overcast cloud conditions and visibility of 10 miles.

The Archer's performance charts indicated that 75 percent power at 6500 feet would require about 10 gallons per hour and the time en route from New Haven to Biddeford would be 1.5 hours. The pilot figured he'd arrive with 34 gallons remaining, good for at least three hours of air time and more than enough to get home.

The northbound trip was uneventful. On the ground at Biddeford, the fuel gauges and a visual inspection of the tanks confirmed the fuel remaining, so the pilot elected not to top off before heading home.

In a statement after the accident (edited slightly for length), he said, "The weather briefing I received from Bangor FSS reported winds aloft at 6000 to be light and variable. As this was my planned altitude, I figured the trip would take no more than two hours en route from Biddeford to New Haven. Using the 75 percent power numbers I would have enough fuel to get to New Haven plus 30 minutes to my alternate and thereafter for at least another 45 minutes."

That appears to have been a legal fuel load for the trip; enough to get to the airport of first intended landing, plus enough to fly to the alternate, plus another 45 minutes at cruise power. But it didn't take into account any ATC delays, unforecast weather nor clearance amendments that might increase the flight time. (I don't know what your experience has been, but I could count on the fingers of one hand the clearance amendments that have shortened a trip!) The 34 gallons in this airplane would be enough if everything went as planned on the way home.

The passenger finished his business in Biddeford at midday and the pilot was ready to go. He had filed an IFR flight plan, requesting V-3/V-16 to Norwich (ORW), V-475 to Madison (MAD), direct New Haven. This route was 210 miles and should have taken a bit more than one hour and a half to fly. It also traversed the very heart of Boston Logan International Airport airspace at 6000 feet. The pilot checked in with Pease AFB Approach Control about 10 minutes after takeoff. Within one minute, things began to change:

Pilot: Good afternoon Pease, Cherokee One-Five-Nine-One-Seven is with you level at 6000.
ATC: November-One-Five-Nine-One-Seven, Pease Approach, you're loud and clear, the altimeter 30.37.

The pilot couldn't hear it, but there was a lot of interphone chatter as the Pease controller and his counterpart in Boston Approach worked out a new route for the Cherokee. Going overhead Boston at 6000 feet just wasn't going to work. And then, the words we all hate to hear:

ATC: Warrior Nine-One-Seven, I have an amendment to your clearance, proceed direct Exalt [intersection] via Victor 139.
Pilot: Say again for Nine-One-Seven?
ATC: Nine-One-Seven, proceed direct Exalt via Victor 139 and I'll have the rest of your clearance in a moment.
Pilot: Okay, direct Exalt via Victor 139.

At this point, a couple of things were apparent. First, the amended routing was farther to the east and therefore would take longer. Second, Victor 139 would take the Cherokee over water, well beyond comfortable gliding distance from land. The process of route or altitude negotiation should have begun right then and there.

Ten minutes later, after a short vector for traffic, the Pease controller offered the rest of the routing:

ATC: Warrior Nine-One-Seven, I have an amendment to your clearance, advise ready to copy.
Pilot: Nine-One-Seven is ready to copy.
ATC: Nine-One-Seven is cleared present position to New Haven via direct Sandy Point [VOR], the Sandy Point 284 radial Cream [intersection], direct, maintain 6000.
Pilot: Okay, we're cleared to New Haven, direct Sandy Point, then the Sandy Point 284 radial...I lost it after that.

ATC: Warrior Nine-One-Seven, roger, after the Sandy Point 284 radial, Cream, direct.
Pilot: Okay, Sandy Point 284 radial Cream, direct, maintain six.
ATC: Warrior Nine-One-Seven, readback correct, contact Boston Approach 118.25.

Victor 139 lies mostly over water (over 50 miles) from the time it leaves Kennebunk VOR until it makes landfall southeast of Boston. Setting aside for the moment the increase in a pilot's pucker-factor in a single-engine airplane at low altitude with not even a life jacket on board, consider the increased distance. The amended routing amounted to an additional 44 miles (at least another 20 minutes flying time). The new routing would clearly take a significant bite out of the Cherokee's bare-minimum fuel reserve.

Still No Sweat

The next hour or so must have been completely uneventful, because the NTSB report contains no reference to communications as the Cherokee passed through Boston's airspace. When the pilot turned the corner at Sandy Point, he was handed off to New York Approach and the conversation indicated an uncomfortable situation was shaping up:

Pilot: Good afternoon, New York, Cherokee One-Five-Nine-One-Seven is with you, level at 6000.
ATC: Cherokee One-Five-Nine-One-Seven, roger, expect vectors for the ILS Runway 2 at New Haven<193>make that the visual for 20 at New Haven. Lima is current.
Pilot: Could I have, ah, you got the current weather at New Haven?
ATC: Yeah, it's VFR, visibility eight miles, wind 20 at 6, altimeter 30.03.
Pilot: Yeah, we'd appreciate direct as possible, ah, we're getting a little low on fuel.
ATC: Proceed direct New Haven.
Pilot: Direct New Haven, roger.

Something's wrong here. The Cherokee had been in the air one hour and 36 minutes. There was 34 gallons of gas in the tanks at takeoff. At the planned consumption of 10 gallons per hour, there should have been enough gas remaining to fly at least another hour and a half. Nevertheless, only 25 miles from New Haven, the pilot said, "We're getting a little low on fuel."

The pilot's post-accident statement to NTSB gives a good understanding of the situation: "Between Boston and Sandy Point we smelled gas a few times, but only briefly, and with the engine running fine, not much though was given to this. As we neared Providence, I now recall looking at the gauges because we once again smelled fuel. The fuel gauges read lower than what they should but not overly—right tank approximately 10 gallons and left tank 5-6 gallons."

The fuel gauges should have indicated 15 gallons after landing at New Haven, not when the Cherokee passed Providence 30 minutes ago.

There was clearly a major problem in either fuel consumption or the fuel gauges. The pilot's statement explains why he declared a low fuel state: "Shortly after listening to the ATIS at New Haven, the engine started losing power. I immediately went through an emergency procedure checklist which involved switching tanks, and that did the trick [restored power]. I had just been handed over to New York Approach, so after checking the fuel situation (5 gallons right and 5-6 gallons left) asked for direct New Haven due to a possible fuel problem."

By now the Cherokee was only 18-20 miles from New Haven. Three minutes after getting that fix from the controller, the pilot was cleared to descend to 4000 feet. The pilot accepted, giving up valuable altitude in a situation whose outcome might well depend on squeezing every foot of gliding distance from the airplane.

Eleven minutes after "we're getting a little low on fuel," the hammer fell:

ATC: Okay, somebody else just called in, stepped on me, say again. Is that Nine-One-Seven, you're level four?
Pilot: Yes sir, we're level four, we're losing fuel pressure. We're going to need vectors to somewhere.
ATC: Okay, Calverton Airport is off your 10 o'clock and 10 miles, you want to go there? Or Suffolk is off your 9 o'clock and 12 miles. You want to go there?
Pilot: Closest place<193>and we're about to lose our engine here.
ATC: Okay, Nine-One-Seven, turn left to a heading of 230.
Pilot: Left to 230, roger.
ATC: November Nine-One-Seven, do you have the approach plates for Peconic [Calverton] Airport?
Pilot: That's affirmative, sir. We just lost our engine.
ATC: You have a dead engine right now. Do you want to land Peconic? I could put you right on the final. Fly heading of 230, intercept the Calverton 057 radial.
Pilot: 057, roger.
ATC: Nine-One-Seven, at your discretion, sir, descend and maintain 2000 for the approach.

Pilot: Cleared down to 2000, roger.

The Cherokee continued its glide for the next two minutes and was just about established on the final approach course when the pilot reported breaking out into visual conditions.

ATC: Cherokee Nine-One-Seven, verify you are in IFR conditions.
Pilot: We just broke out into vmc.
ATC: You have just broke out of the clouds, you said?
Pilot: That's affirmative, sir, we're not going, ah, we're not going to make the shore out here.
ATC: Okay, how about off your 10 o'clock, ah correction 12 o'clock and seven miles is Peconic and ah, do you have it in sight? About 8 o'clock and five miles there's a small airport, Mattituck Airport.
Pilot: We're never going to make the shore out here, we're going to go for Mattituck.
ATC: Cherokee Nine-One-Seven, radar contact is lost. We are advising Coast Guard at this time.
Pilot: Nine-One-Seven, thanks.

That was the last radio communication. The pilot headed for an offshore oil platform, but there just wasn't enough energy left in the airplane. The Cherokee hit the water a couple of miles from the north shore of Long Island. Both occupants got out without injuries. The airplane stayed afloat for 15-20 minutes. Although rescue helicopters passed close by on several occasions, the pilot and his passenger weren't spotted. After three hours in the water, the pilot elected to make for the shore and was eventually picked up by a rescue helicopter. The passenger was never seen again.

The Fuel-Burn Mystery

A Cherokee Warrior should burn 9-10 gallons per hour at 75 percent power and this one was probably doing just that. The key here is fuel burn, not fuel consumption, because it's obvious that some fuel was leaving the tanks but not going through the engine.

The pilot's mention of smelling fuel on several occasions throughout the return flight is significant and NTSB investigators looked into the history of the airplane. It was discovered that this Cherokee had a tendency to use more fuel than normal. Since it was used predominantly for training and local flights, the tanks were almost always topped off and few pilots flew it on trips long enough to use most of the fuel.

Several writeups surfaced during the investigation, one of which dealt with a pilot's complaint that the fuel gauges indicated roughly 20 percent too high...a dangerous situation. Another pilot said he always flight-planned this airplane for a fuel burn of 13 gallons per hour. Probably not at all by accident, that was almost exactly the consumption rate on the flight that wound up with this Cherokee in the drink.

The airplane still rests on the bottom of Long Island Sound, so no one has been able to check the condition of the fuel selector valve. But we can conclude there must have been a considerable leak when the pilot selected the right tank, which is when the smell of fuel became apparent and that fuel was being lost overboard.

The combination of fuel gauge errors on the hazardous side and complaints of super-high consumption should have initiated an inspection that didn't stop until the problem was resolved. As the pilot said, Under normal circumstances in that model aircraft, that problem [fuel exhaustion] should not have arisen...and we agree.

What We Learned

There weren't normal circumstances and there are at least three areas in this scenario that can be very educational.

First, never trust fuel gauges. The engineering problems, e.g., shallow tanks and wing dihedral, make it difficult to provide a completely accurate and reliable measurement system. That is unless the manufacturer throws a lot of money at the problem and most single-engine airplanes aren't so endowed. Never rely totally on system integrity in airplanes you don't really know. Are you willing to place complete trust in other pilots' squawks and in the operator taking care of them properly?

Second, unless an overload rears its head, never pass up a chance to top the tanks. Particularly when you're facing an IFR journey through busy airspace and there's just enough fuel in the tanks to comply with the regulations, it makes sense to refuel. "I have an amendment to your clearance" is something you should plan for and expect.

Third, when a controller issues a new routing or altitude that you don't want, turn it down. The PIC is responsible for the safe conduct of the flight, not the controller. The FARs give you authority to refuse an unacceptable clearance. If you don't want to fly over water, don't do it. There's always another way to go.

Finally, if you should ever find yourself in a situation that even hints at fuel exhaustion, don't give up one single foot of altitude until absolutely necessary. For a glider pilot, altitude is like money in the bank.

• Section Two •

ATC's Role

Controller
Error

F ortunately, the nation's air traffic controllers are a
highly trained, very capable group of individuals.
That training, plus the structure of the rules and
regulations under which they work, means that accidents which are directly
contributed to by a controller's foul-up are exceedingly rare.
That doesn't mean they don't happen, however.

A Moment of Inattention

When the weather is IMC, you file an IFR flight plan and someone else
assumes responsibility for aircraft separation while you're in clouds.

Someone else is the air traffic controller. At first blush, an instrument
pilot might believe that he or she can put on blinders, follow ATC
instructions to the letter, and arrive safely every time. Controllers are
people too, subject to all the human errors that plague the pilot
population. The situation we're going to discuss focuses on the relationship between instrument pilots and controllers. It should make
you acutely aware of some responsibilities you may have taken for
granted when flying in clouds.

Flight to Salinas

A Beech Baron departed a private airport 35 miles southwest of Fresno,
California on a routine IFR trip to deliver three passengers to Salinas,
California. In command of the flight was a professional pilot with an
ATP certificate, 33 years old, and 7600 hours as a pilot (of which nearly
half were in the Baron). He had only 262 hours of instrument time (less
than four percent of his total), which may have contributed to the

outcome.

The Salinas Airport is east of Monterey Bay and is situated at the head of a long, narrow northwest-southeast valley. As you approach Salinas from the southeast, the Gabilan Range is on the right and the Santa Lucia Range is on the left. Although the valley widens as it nears the sea, there are 2000- and 3000-foot ridges within ten miles of the airport.

On the day of the accident, Salinas weather was 1000 broken, 3000 overcast, eight miles in light rain and wind from the west at 13 knots. We join the communications when the Baron was 20 miles southeast of Panoche VOR.

Center: Ah, Baron Two-Eight-Delta-Whiskey, now cleared direct Salinas, maintain 8000.
N28DW: Roger, direct Salinas, maintain eight, Delta-Whiskey.

Shortly thereafter, the Baron was handed-off to the next controller who established radar contact, issued the Salinas altimeter and asked the pilot which approach procedure he'd prefer.

N28DW: Okay, due to the altitude we'll have to lose, and since they have a fairly high ceiling, we'll go ahead for the VOR to Runway 13.

Delta-Whiskey was then cleared for a pilot's discretion descent to 7000 feet. Four minutes passed as the Baron proceeded to the Salinas VOR, then a potential traffic conflict appeared on radar.

Center: Two-Eight-Delta-Whiskey, Oakland, turn left heading 230, vectors around traffic.
N28DW: Delta-Whiskey, left 230.

N28DW entered Monterey Approach Control's airspace and a routine hand-off was effected. Landline communications between the controllers went like this:

Oakland: Five northeast of Gonza, flying a heading of 230 now, Baron Two-Eight-Delta-Whiskey, and he's at seven thousand.
Monterey: I've got to find the strip on him, going to Salinas. Okay, here it is, Baron Two-Eight-Delta-Whiskey, level at seven, heading 230, radar contact, our control. Have him contact me on 120.8.

Northwest or Northeast?

It was a routine hand-off except for one thing; when the Center controller said that N28DW was five miles northwest of the Gonza Intersection, the airplane was actually five miles northeast of Gonza. Another airplane was at that moment five northwest of Gonza (a Swearingen commuter flight headed for San Francisco). Its track was roughly the same as the Baron's, but altitude (descending from FL180 to 6000 feet) and groundspeed (84 knots greater than the Baron) were remarkably different, conditions which went completely unnoticed by both controllers.

Now wait a minute. Don't transponder targets give controllers information about squawk-code, altitude and groundspeed? They sure do, normally. But in one of those circumstances that causes some folks to believe in good and bad Karma, that portion of the equipment had been removed from the Monterey facility an hour and a half earlier. Therefore, only primary and beacon target returns were depicted.

Over the next several minutes, the two airplanes continued on parallel courses; the Swearingen northwestbound to the left of the Salinas Airport and the Baron to the right. The pilot of N28DW earlier requested the VOR 13 approach, which requires a series of right turns to the final approach course. After a positioning vector of 340 degrees, the controller set the Baron to intercept the final approach course.

Monterey: Baron Two-Eight-Delta-Whiskey, Monterey, turn right heading 090, maintain at or above two thousand until established on the final approach course, cleared for the approach.
N28DW: Two-Eight-Delta-Whiskey, roger, right heading 090, maintain two thousand until established, cleared for the approach.

The controller noticed that the target didn't turn, which is understandable, since he wasn't talking to the Swearingen and wasn't looking at the blip which was the Baron. When it became apparent that the radar target he was following was on a northwesterly track, he inquired of the Baron:

Monterey: Baron Two-Eight-Delta-Whiskey, say your heading.
N28DW: Okay, we're heading 090.
Monterey: Ah, Two-Eight-Delta-Whiskey, ah, are you in that turn now? (The controller's voice is filled with uncertainty).
N28DW: Affirmative.
Monterey: (After a short pause). Ah, what do you show from the Salinas VOR, ah, I'm questioning my identification here. The target I had is continuing, ah, northwest.
N28DW: (No response).

Monterey: Baron Two-Eight-Delta-Whiskey, Monterey, give me your radial off Salinas and your altitude now, please.
N28DW: (No response to this transmission, or any of the others that followed in the next few minutes. The Baron had crashed into one of the ridges east of the airport.)

An extensive investigation was launched after the accident, including a check of the radar equipment and the controllers themselves. After all was said and done, it was concluded that the controllers misidentified the Baron's target and that error was carried forward when the flight was handed off to Monterey Approach.

Against All Odds?

The odds of the radar equipment out for maintenance, two airplanes traveling on parallel tracks, controller confusion and pilot lack of awareness coming together like this are surely astronomical.

The air traffic control system's contribution to this accident may not be easy to justify, but the human errors are easy to understand. Not so clear is why the pilot didn't suspect that something was wrong and that's of primary concern to those of use who try to learn from these accidents. Let's consider the pilot's role in more detail.

At some point in the flight, the pilot set up his nav radios to take him to the Salinas VOR. This probably occurred when the flight was cleared direct to Salinas. The Baron was equipped with RNAV and the settings found in the wreckage were 39 miles and 250 degrees (the waypoint address for Salinas using the Panoche VOR.)

The pilot may have intended to use the RNAV display for the approach. That's not quite legal, since he was not cleared for an RNAV procedure, but that's just a technicality (the information on the panel would have been the same).

On the other hand, the Baron's RNAV may have worked only on the #2 nav indicator, and the pilot would have selected the Salinas VOR on the #1 set for the approach. Which of these configurations will never be known and it really doesn't matter, since either way there was ample information available about the airplane's position as it approached the airport.

The last two vectors issued to the Baron (300 degrees, then 340 degrees) placed the airplane well to the right of the VOR and to the right of the approach course. If we assume that the pilot made no changes to the OBS setting on the RNAV display, the course indicator would have moved conspicuously to the left as the airplane passed to the right of the waypoint.

If we further assume that the pilot had set his #1 nav indicator (an HSI) for the approach (with the course selector on 122 degrees), the course deviation indicator on this instrument would also have been displaced to the left. These were two indications that the airplane was well to the right of the final approach course.

It is not usual for an airplane approaching Salinas from the southeast to be vectored in that area for an approach. As a matter of fact, local controllers testified that they frequently used the airspace in the northeast for that purpose, provided that there was sufficient altitude for terrain clearance. So the set-up for the approach might have appeared routine to the pilot at this point.

Now comes the critical moment, the pilot's last chance to figure that where he was vectored was not where he wanted to go. The final vector, intended to turn the airplane onto the final approach course, was a right turn to 090 degrees. This heading was to be maintained until established on the 302 radial.

That's a good vector for an airplane on the other side of the approach course, but a fatal one for the Baron. A pilot knowledgeable of position, and familiar with the terrain surrounding the Salinas Airport, would surely have questioned a turn to the east, knowing that such a course would eventually lead into the high terrain.

Know The Terrain

There are several lessons to be learned from this accident. First, any vector should be accepted only when you, the pilot, are sure that it won't fly you into trouble. Don't depend totally on someone else when you're descending or maneuvering close to the ground.

You'd have to work hard to get into this kind of trouble during an approach to someplace like Indianapolis, where the terrain is as flat as a billiard table. However, when approaching a valley airport, your altitude awareness should be extremely high.

Second, set up your nav displays as early as practical during an approach. This usually is as soon as you no longer need the displays to get where you're going. When the controller issues vectors to get you lined up for the approach, tune, identify and position the course selector to the approach numbers.

This procedure assumes that virtually all IFR airplanes are equipped with two VOR receivers, making it possible to monitor airplane position with the #2 unit. You only have one VOR? There's usually a close-by NDB, or commercial broadcast station that can furnish a position to keep you generally aware.

Finally, always pay attention to your position. No vector or clearance should be a surprise at this point in an IFR flight. You should have a good idea of what will happen next. If a controller wants you to do something that doesn't look right, speak up. A discreet inquiry sure beats the socks off trying to move a mountain with your airplane!

Overriding
The Controller

I t doesn't happen often, but it's a safe bet most of us have been forgotten by a controller at one time or another. Normally, of course, it's not a problem: Either the controller realizes the gaffe and corrects it, or the pilot starts asking questions.

Which brings us to the following accident. At what point should a pilot step over the authority line and say no to the controller?

An Airplane Running Downhill

Pilots are highly motivated to do as the controller instructs: It's what makes the system work. By the same token, controllers are highly trained to issue correct, sensible and timely instructions, which is what keeps traffic flowing smoothly and safely.

The FARs make it crystal clear that we should follow the controller's instructions, but they also make clear that we have the authority to decline if necessary. The key lies in recognizing that what the controller is telling us to do isn't quite right.

In this accident, the controller goofed, and let an airplane fly right through the glideslope without issuing an approach clearance. The pilot goofed too: Instead of promptly blowing the whistle, instead obeyed the hasty directions that followed, making an unstabilized approach that ended short of the runway.

The Setup

It was a January night in Jacksonville, Florida; measured ceiling 300 feet, visibility one mile in light rain. Jacksonville Approach Control was routinely vectoring flights to the ILS Runway 07.

Cheyenne N700CM departed an airport southeast of Atlanta, bound for Jacksonville to drop off a passenger. The pilot held a private certificate with multi-engine and instrument ratings; a first-class medical and 1700 hours of flight time. He had 100 hours in the Cheyenne, which included a formal course of flight and ground training.

The radio communications begin as 700CM calls Jacksonville Approach 40 miles northwest of the airport.

700CM: Jacksonville, Cheyenne Seven-Hundred-Charlie-Mike at one-two thousand.
Approach: Cheyenne Seven-Hundred-Charlie-Mike, Jacksonville, one-two thousand, verify you got information alpha.
700CM: Seven-Hundred-Charlie-Mike, that's affirm.
Approach: Roger, and the Runway 07 RVR is more than six thousand.

In the next eight minutes, the Cheyenne was cleared to 3000 feet and vectored to a downwind for the ILS. The controller noticed that 700CM was closing in on the airplane in front of him and asked for a speed reduction to 150 knots. The pilot complied.

The Cheyenne was vectored to a base leg. As the airplane approached the localizer:

Approach: Cheyenne Seven-Hundred-Charlie-Mike, turn left heading 090, join the final approach course and track inbound. Maintain three thousand.
700CM: Charlie-Mike, roger, 090 and join the localizer inbound.

Thirty seconds later, the controller issued a traffic advisory:

Approach: Seven-Hundred-Charlie-Mike, there's traffic at 12 to 1 o'clock and five miles, a Boeing 727 out of three thousand, descending. He'll be on the approach ahead of you.
700CM: Seven-Hundred-Charlie-Mike, we won't be able to see him.
Approach: Okay, are you IMC at this time?

The pilot didn't answer the question, but you can assume he couldn't see the traffic because of weather. This over the top vectoring is not unusual, but there's a potential for wake turbulence for the overflown airplane.

When the traffic advisory was issued, the Cheyenne was intercepting the localizer about 15 miles from the airport, level at 3000 feet and at 150 knots. Take special notice of the pilot's clearance, "...join the final approach course, track inbound, maintain three thousand."

This was intended to get the Cheyenne in line with other traffic and should have been followed at the appropriate time with a clearance for the ILS itself.

Let's stop for a moment and analyze the situation. At 15 miles, the pilot would have the localizer tuned and identified (the intercept and track inbound were normal). At this distance, the glideslope needle would have been fully deflected to indicate that the airplane was still well below the glideslope. The glideslope needle would have given a fly down indication approximately 12 miles out.

The glideslope intercept altitude is 1900 feet msl. Not only had the controller failed to issue an approach clearance, there was no clearance to a lower altitude to intercept the glideslope. The warning flags should have flown in the pilot's mind and he should have questioned the clearance; if not as the localizer was intercepted, then certainly as the glideslope needle moved off the peg and started to drop.

The controller was preoccupied with another matter, and six minutes after his last conversation with 700CM, Jacksonville Tower noticed something amiss and called the approach controller:

Tower: Ah, Charlie-Mike never descended. I guess you know that.
Approach: Okay. (Guess what other two words he said at this point).
Approach: Cheyenne Seven-Hundred-Charlie-Mike, ah, you're cleared for the approach. Tower now on 118.3.

As this was taking place, Charlie-Mike continued inbound at 3000 feet and 150 knots. Six seconds later, the pilot called the tower. Two calls were required because the controllers were talking frantically to each other.

Remember the B-727 that was cleared over the top of 700CM? It was slowed to 130 knots and the Cheyenne was closing rapidly.

Tower: Seven-Hundred-Charlie-Mike, roger, I show you about half a mile west of the marker. Descend as published on the approach sir.
700CM: Seven-Hundred-Charlie-Mike.
Tower: Yes sir, are you still showing at 3000?
700CM: Seven-Hundred-Charlie-Mike (unintelligible).

Another controller, the coordinator between approach control and the tower, got into the act:

Coord: (Addressing the tower) You got Charlie-Mike yet?
Tower: Yeah, I'm gonna break him off. It don't look good to me. My problem is he's doing 40 knots faster than Eastern [the 727 in front of the Cheyenne]. I'll keep him. I'll run him in.
Coord: Just wait and see what happens. You know, see if it works out.
Tower: Okay.

Forty seconds later, the tower saw that the Cheyenne was still gaining on the Eastern 727 and was concerned about the separation.

Tower: Seven-Hundred-Charlie-Mike, if practical, reduce your speed. Traffic on the runway is an Eastern jet, hasn't cleared yet.
700CM: Seven-Hundred-Charlie-Mike.
Tower: Thank you, sir. You're two and three-quarters miles from the runway right now.
700CM: Seven-Hundred-Charlie-Mike.

The controllers discussed what they were going to do with Charlie-Mike if the approach was missed. Twenty seconds later, the tower cleared the Cheyenne to land. The pilot acknowledged the clearance and wasn't heard from again. The Cheyenne hit the ground a half-mile from the runway. Both occupants were killed.

Wake Turbulence Possible?

The proximity of the Cheyenne to the Eastern 727 was investigated. An NTSB engineering report indicated:

The ground plot indicates that 700CM would not have crossed the flight path of the 727 until about four seconds prior to ground contact or at about 200 feet above the ground. The vertical velocity would have been about 4000 feet per minute [descent] during this time, which was the first opportunity for 700CM to have been exposed to wake turbulence.
    Also, the fact that the airplane hit wings level tends to indicate that the airplane was not affected by any external upsetting forces such as a wake vortex encounter three to four seconds prior to ground contact.

Vertical Profile

The NTSB created a plot of the Cheyenne's vertical profile from outside the LOM until impact. At first glance, the airplane appears to have executed a steep descent, then a level-off; whereupon it plunged again, leveled-off a second time and dove into the ground.
    The NTSB's vertical profile was compressed and exaggerated the

airplane's vertical excursions. When the plot was stretched out to its real dimensions, it appeared that the pitch excursions weren't that wild. The pilot was trying hard, but never got on the glideslope.

Speed Changes

Two investigators believed that the pilot pushed the nose down to salvage the approach at the controller's urging. The airplane was probably in a clean configuration since the groundspeed increased to 160 knots and the controller commented, "He's doing 40 knots faster than Eastern."

Shortly thereafter, the pilot probably realized that he would need to lower the landing gear and slowed the airplane. The maximum gear-extension speed for the Cheyenne is 156 knots. With this assumption, the next flat spot on the descent profile occurred when the controller asked the pilot to slow because the Eastern 727 was on the runway.

The radar plot shows a ground speed of 140 knots at this point, a slight increase in altitude, then steadily decreasing speed until the airplane hit the ground.

If the pilot pulled the power levers all the way back to comply with the controller's request, the props may have gone into flat pitch (which is characteristic of the PT-6 powerplant). If this occurred, drag would have increased and the airplane hit the ground before the pilot could recover.

A stall or near-stall may have also occurred in the final seconds of this flight.

It Could Have Been Averted

The controller should not have forgotten about 700CM. When the problem became apparent, the controller should have questioned the pilot's ability to continue the approach. When the separation between the Cheyenne and the Eastern 727 became questionable, the controller should have exercised his prerogative and issued missed approach instructions.

On the other hand, the pilot should have noticed that something was amiss when he flew through the glideslope at 3000 feet. He should have queried the controller about being at that altitude. He should have refused the approach clearance and missed the approach when it was apparent that he was not going to intercept the glideslope.

He should have packed it in when the controller said, "...700 Charlie-Mike, if practical reduce your speed. Traffic on the runway ..." Too many things were wrong.

Reluctance to Miss?

The speed increase during the initial descent probably set the stage. The faster the airplane went, the faster the glideslope fell out from under it.

At 160 knots, a 853 fpm rate of descent is required to stay on a three-degree glideslope. When you start 1100 feet high and attempt to capture it, a 1300 fpm descent rate is needed. But that won't solve the problem either, since the glideslope needle will center as you hit the runway.

When the pilot slowed to extend the gear, the airplane leveled off and went above the glideslope. When the controller asked for a slowdown for traffic, the same thing happened again, which worsened the situation.

It makes sense to miss a faulted approach, whether the mistake is yours or the controller's. It takes considerable experience to recognize a bad set of circumstances and to ask a controller, What's going on?

When the answer is not satisfactory, exercise your PIC authority and do something else, which should have been a missed approach.

Be alert for incomplete clearances and instructions. Controllers make mistakes and will continue to do so. Don't become a victim because you didn't speak up.

Confusion On All Sides

This well-publicized accident isn't strictly speaking, the fault of ATC (actually, in this case a Flight Service Specialist). It's equally due to flight crew confusion over a fairly basic point of IFR procedure.

The culprit is the IFR departure procedure. It's the set of written instructions found on certain Jepp plates and at the front of NOS approach plate books.

As we'll see, the briefer apparently did not know what an IFR departure procedure actually is. Both he and the crew were confused about the difference between an IFR departure procedure and a Standard Instrument Departure, or SID. They never did get it straight. This seemingly trivial point caused a fatal accident.

An IFR What?

Departing an airport toward mountainous terrain in the wee hours of the morning ended in disaster for two pilots and their passengers. Repeated calls to flight service to clarify confusion over departure terminology, failure to maintain adequate terrain clearance after take-off and concern about entering a TCA without a clearance were elements in the crash of a Hawker Siddley HS-125 bizjet in March, 1991 near San Diego, CA. The lessons from this accident point out the need to plan a night takeoff carefully, especially in unfamiliar territory.

The accident received a lot of attention since the passengers were members of country singer Reba McEntire's band. Having arrived on the Hawker from Tennessee at 3:30 in the afternoon, they were going to return after an evening concert. The San Diego weather was clear, with 10 miles visibility and calm winds.

Confused Terminology

At 11:20 p.m., the Hawker pilot called the San Diego Flight Service Station and filed an IFR flight plan from San Diego Brown Field to Amarillo, TX with a proposed departure time of midnight. Since the Brown Field Control Tower was closed, the FSS briefer said:

Briefer: Give San Diego Radio a call on this line for your clearance.
Pilot: Can I get airborne out of here?
Briefer: If you can depart VFR, I can get a frequency to pick your clearance up in the air.

Then, the following conversation ensued:

Briefer: I'll call approach and get your frequency. Are you familiar with the Brown Field Departure, sir?
Pilot: No, not really.
Briefer: It should be in your charts. Let me read it to you because they're very particular on the departures. (Brief pause.) Let's see here....
Pilot: It would be in a SID.

So far, so good. All SIDs have names and numbers, but the pilot had no real reason to believe that the briefer wasn't referring to a SID.

Briefer: It's in the SID, yeah. Just a second. I think it's in the STAR, but let's see.

We can see here that the briefer hasn't a clue about the procedure. He's looking for it amongst the Standard Terminal Arrival Routes (STARs).

Pilot: SIDS (unintelligible) government ones are right behind (unintelligible).
Briefer: Takeoff minimums.
Pilot: No, no, you're in the wrong area.
Briefer: Pardon?
Pilot: They're right where the approach plates are for the field.

The pilot then said he would look it up in his own charts. The conversation ended after the briefer gave the pilot a frequency to pick up his clearance after takeoff.

If you're confused about this conversation, you should be. The briefer was referring to the instrument departure procedure (IDP) for Brown Field, but never referred to it by the proper name, so the pilot thought the briefer was referring to a special SID for Brown Field. IDPs are listed with the takeoff minimums in the front of every NOS chart book, whereas SID charts are printed with the approach charts for a particular airport.

Second call
When the pilot said he would look it up, he was referring to a SID. But the confusion didn't end there. At 11:53 p.m., the pilot again called flight service and spoke to the same briefer:

Pilot: I went out there and looked in the California approach plates as far as some sort of special SID out of here. I show absolutely nothing.
Briefer: Okay, let me find it for you and I'll read it to you because they are very particular how you depart.
Briefer: I have a hard time finding it in here. I think it's in this STAR and....
Pilot: Would it be in the STAR as a SID? [What? He's confused as the briefer, now—Ed.]
Briefer: Yeah, as a SID. I know it's funny but....
Pilot: I didn't think to look at the STAR.

There's no reason he should have. He should, however, have realized the briefer wasn't talking about a SID, and considered the only other sort of departure information there is: The IDP.

Again, the briefer was looking up the correct departure procedure for Brown Field, but referred to it incorrectly, which only further confused the pilot. After further discussion, the briefer read the correct IDP for Runway 08L at Brown Field: *Turn left direct PGY Vortac to cross at or above 1500. Continue climb on PGY R-270 to intercept MZB Vortac R-160 at or above 3000, continue direct MZB Vortac via R-160.*

The briefer also read the IDP for Runway 26R: *Climbing right turn heading 280, cross MZB Vortac R-130 at or above 1500 and intercept MZB Vortac R-160 at or above 3000 direct MZB Vortac.*

The pilot replied, "Okay, that'll do me," and hung up.

Notice that both departure procedures take you north and west of the airport, away from the mountains to the east (more on this later).

Third Discussion
At 12:28 a.m., the San Diego FSS briefer found himself talking to the Hawker pilot once again:

Pilot: I have looked that up and I do have that in the STAR section or

C7

 TAKE-OFF MINS

90347

NAME	TAKE-OFF MINIMUMS

SACRAMENTO, CA
SACRAMENTO EXECUTIVE
TAKE-OFF MINIMUMS: **Rwy 2,** ½ mile,
FAR 135. **Rwy 12,** 300-1
DEPARTURE PROCEDURE: Climb direct to SAC
VORTAC.

SALINAS, CA
SALINAS MUNI
TAKE-OFF MINIMUMS: **Rwys 3, 14, 21, 32,** NA.
Rwy 31, RVR/24, FAR 135.
Rwy 8, Categories C, D, 3600-2 or std. with
min. climb of 420' per NM to 4100. **Rwy 13,**
Categories C, D, 3600-2 or std. with min. climb
of 500' per NM to 4000.
DEPARTURE PROCEDURE: **Rwys 8, 13, 26,** turn
right. Climb on SNS R-275 to 4100. **Rwy 31,**
turn left. Climb on SNS R-275 to 4100. **Rwy 8,**
2000, then climbing right turn to cross SNS
VORTAC at of above 3000.

SAN DIEGO, CA
BROWN FIELD MUNI
TAKE-OFF MINIMUMS: **Rwys 8L/R,** Categories
A, B, 1800-1 or std. with min. climb of 420' per
NM to 2400; Categories C, D, 3100-2 or std. with
min. climb of 500' per NM to 3900.
DEPARTURE PROCEDURE: Comply with radar
vectors, or: **Rwys 8L/R,** turn left climb direct PGY
VORTAC to cross at or above 1500. Continue
climb on PGY R-270 to intercept MZB VORTAC
R-160 at or above 3000, continue direct MZB
VORTAC via R-160. **Rwys 26L/R,** climbing right
turn heading 280, cross MZB VORTAC R-130 at
or above 1500 and intercept MZB VORTAC R-160
at or above 3000 direct MZB VORTAC.

MONTGOMERY FIELD
TAKE-OFF MINIMUMS: **Rwy 5,** 1300-2 or std.
with min. climb of 300' per NM to 2000. **Rwy 23,**
400-1 or std. with min. climb 220' per NM to 700.
DEPARTURE PROCEDURE: Comply with radar
vectors, or: **Rwy 5, 10L/R, 23,** turn right heading
270. **Rwy 28L/R,** turn left heading 250. Intercept
V-23, V-25, V-27, V-363 continue climb via,
assigned airway.

SAN DIEGO INTL-LINDBERGH FIELD
TAKE-OFF MINIMUMS: **Rwy 9,** 1100-2 or 500-1
with min. climb of 440' per NM to 1400. **Rwy 13,**
600-1 or std. with min. climb of 480' per NM to
1400. **Rwys 27, 31,** 400-1 or std. with min. climb
of 320' per NM to 500.
DEPARTURE PROCEDURE: Comply with SID or
radar vectors, or; All departures climb direct
MZB VORTAC then via assigned airway.

NAME	TAKE-OFF MINIMUMS

SAN DIEGO (EL CAJON), CA
GILLESPIE FIELD
TAKE-OFF MINIMUMS: **Rwys 9L/R,** Categories
A, B, 1400-2; Categories C, D, 1800-2 or 500-1½
with min. climb of 400' per NM to 2200. **Rwys 17,
27L/R, 35,** 1400-2 or 400-1 with min. climb of
400' per NM to 2200.
TAKEOFF MINIMUMS FOR RADAR VECTORS:
Rwys 9L/R, 17, 3300-2 or 900-1½ with min.
climb of 420' per NM to 4200. **Rwys 27L/R, 35,**
3300-2 or 400-1 with min. climb of 400' per NM
to 4200.
DEPARTURE PROCEDURE: Comply with radar
vectors or: **Rwys 9L/R, 27L/R,** turn right.
Rwy 35, turn left. All aircraft climb heading 165
to intercept MZB VORTAC R-076 westbound, cross
MZB VORTAC at or above MCA for direction of
flight.

SAN FRANCISCO, CA
SAN FRANCISCO INTL
TAKE-OFF MINIMUMS: **Rwys 28L, 28R,** 1000-2
or std. with min. climb of 300' per NM to 1000.
Rwy 19R. Categories A/B, **Rwy 19L,** 1300-2 or
std. with min. climb of 480' per NM to 1400.
Rwy 19R, Categories C/D, 2100-2 or std. with
min. climb of 530' per NM to 1800.
DEPARTURE PROCEDURE: Comply with SID or
radar vectors, or: **Rwys 1L/R, 28L/R,** climb runway
heading to 2000', then climb on course.
Rwys 19L/R, climbing left turn to 2000' to
intercept SFO R-090, then climb on course.
Rwys 10L/R, climb to 2000' via SFO R-090,
then climb on course.

SAN JOSE, CA
SAN JOSE INTL
TAKE-OFF MINIMUMS: **Rwys 11, 12R, 12L,**
2700-2 or std. with climb of 330' per NM to
3200'.
DEPARTURE PROCEDURE: Comply with SID or;
Rwys 29, 30L, 30R, climb to 4000 direct OAK
VORTAC. **Rwys 11, 12L, 12R,** climbing right turn
to 4000 direct OAK VORTAC.

SAN LUIS OBISPO, CA
SAN LUIS OBISPO COUNTY-McCHESNEY FIELD
TAKE-OFF MINIMUMS: **Rwys 7, 25,** NA. **Rwy 11,**
300-2 or std. with a min. climb of 350' per NM
to 3000'. **Rwy 29,** 1300-2 or std. with a min.
climb of 275' per NM to 1700'.
DEPARTURE PROCEDURE: **Rwy 11,** climb runway
heading to 2000 to intercept GLJ R-336 then
climbing right turn to 4000 via GLJ R-336 to join
V27; or comply with published SID. **Rwy 29,** climb
to 4000 via I-SBP LOC west course and PRB R-204
to FRAMS Int; or comply with published SID.

SW-2

 TAKE-OFF MINS

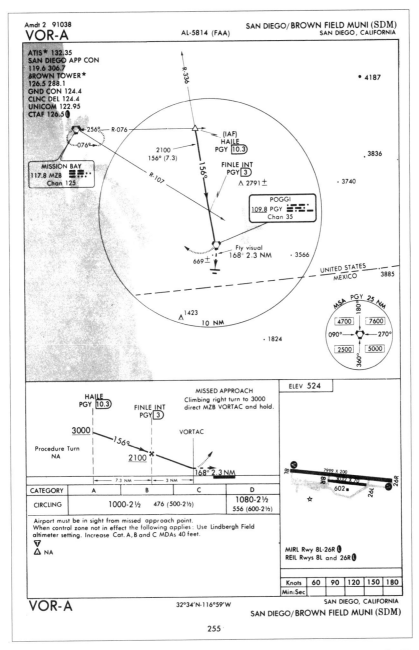

Confusion is often caused by the NOS departure procedure depiction. The T symbol at lower left of the chart tells a pilot to flip to the front of the book, shown at left. The Jepp chart on the next page places the IDP on the airport diagram.

SAN DIEGO, CALIF   **KSDM**   (63-1) APR 14-89   **JEPPESEN**

BROWN MUN

N32 34.3 W116 58.8   167.5°/2.3 From PGY 109.8

Elev **524'**   Var 14°E

*ATIS 132.35	SAN DIEGO Departure (R)
BROWN Clearance 124.4	125.15
Ground 124.4	
*Tower CTAF 126.5	(Limited) VOT 109.0

117-00   116-59   116-58

Rwys 8R & 26R right traffic pattern.

32-35   32-35

Elev 524'

8L ~082°

NORTH DIAGONAL   ARP

Elev 505'

7999'

A   A   8R ~082°   B

3032'   26L ~262°

Elev 518'   Elev 505'

26R ~262°

558'

SOUTH DIAGONAL   Control Tower 602'

32-34   32-34

Feet	0	1000	2000	3000	4000	5000
Meters	0		500	1000		1500

117-00   116-59   116-58

ADDITIONAL RUNWAY INFORMATION

		USABLE LENGTHS LANDING BEYOND			
RWY		Threshold	Glide Slope	TAKE-OFF	WIDTH
8L	❶MIRL ❶REIL ❶AVASI-L				200'
26R	❶MIRL ❶REIL ❶AVASI-L (angle 3.9°)				
8R					70'
26L					

❶ Activate on 126.5 when Twr inop.

TAKE-OFF & IFR DEPARTURE PROCEDURE

Rwys 26L,26R		Rwys 8L,8R					FOR FILING AS ALTERNATE
		CAT A & B AIRCRAFT		**CAT C & D AIRCRAFT**			
Forward Vis Ref	STD	With Mim climb of 420'/NM to 2400'	Other	With Mim climb of 500'/NM to 3900'	Other		
		Forward Vis Ref	STD		Forward Vis Ref	STD	

1 & 2 Eng	¼	1	1	1800-1	¼	1	3100-2	A / B / C / D	NA
3 & 4 Eng	½	½				½			

IFR DEPARTURE PROCEDURE: Comply with radar vectors, or: Rwys 8L/R turn left climb direct PGY VOR to cross at or above 1500'. Continue climb on PGY VOR R-270 to intercept MZB VOR R-160 at or above   3000', continue direct MZB VOR via MZB VOR R-160. Rwys 26L/R climbing right turn heading 280°, cross MZB VOR R-130 at or above 1500' and intercept MZB VOR R-160 at or above 3000' direct MZB VOR.   AMND 1

CHANGES: Lighting activation frequency.

actually in the minimum section. [Was the pilot looking at the Take-Off Minimums section, which is where the IDPs are listed?—Ed.]
Briefer: Right, that's what I said, it's in the STAR, in the arrival section. [Was the briefer confusing the entire front section of the NOS book as the arrival section?—Ed.]

The pilot expressed concern that if he followed the SID, he might enter the San Diego TCA before getting his clearance. The briefer agreed. Then the pilot solicited advice from the briefer on how he should depart.

Pilot: So I would be better off if I headed northeast and stayed down below 3000 [feet].
Briefer: Uh huh.
Pilot: Do you agree on that? [What is the pilot asking a FSS specialist for? The FSS is not ATC!—Ed.]
Briefer: Yeah, sure. That'll be fine.
Pilot: Okay, I just want to check with you on it. I understand that's a normal IFR departure, but I'm going out VFR.
Briefer: That's right. You are going out VFR. I keep forgetting that.

Satisfied he had a plan that would work, the pilot thanked the briefer for his assistance. With the passengers arriving later than expected, the pilot took off at 1:40 a.m. and contacted San Diego Departure:

Pilot: This is Hawker Eight-Three-One-Lima-Charlie just off Brown Field standing by for our IFR to Amarillo.
Approach: Your clearance clocked out here. Let me put it right back in. I'll be right back with you.

As if things weren't bad enough, the ATC computer had kicked out their IFR flight plan since it had been more than 90 minutes past their proposed departure time of midnight. The controller gave N31LC a squawk-code and said, "I'll call you right back."
Moments later, a controller in the tower at North Island Naval Air Station (about 17 miles away) called San Diego Approach:

Tower: I was just watching a VFR squawk off Brown Field and I just noticed a large explosion over that way and the target disappeared from my radar screen.
Approach: Mine also.

N31LC had run into a mountain eight miles northeast of Brown Field at 3300 feet msl. No one survived.

Departure Planning

The Hawker pilot was an ATP with more than 15,000 hours. With this much experience, it's hard to believe he didn't have a better plan to depart an unfamiliar airport safely at night. During the investigation, the crew of another bizjet waiting to depart at the same time told NTSB that the pilot never discussed departure planning with them nor with his co-pilot before walking out to the airplane. Instead, he apparently relied solely on the FSS briefer for departure information.

The Airman's Information Manual gives the following guidance when departing IFR: Each pilot, prior to departing an airport on an IFR flight should consider the type of terrain and other obstacles on or in the vicinity of the departure airport and:

• Determine whether a departure procedure and/or SID is available for obstacle avoidance.

• Determine if obstacle avoidance can be maintained visually or that the departure procedure or SID should be followed.

• Determine what action will be necessary and take such action that will assure a safe departure.

In their initial conversation, the FSS briefer was being helpful by asking the pilot if he was familiar with the Brown Field Departure. We know from the transcript that the pilot thought the briefer was referring to a SID. Brown Field has an instrument departure procedure, but no SID. Yet it took three phone conversations for the briefer and pilot to understand each other since neither of them used the correct terminology to refer to the two procedures.

Often Misunderstood

IDPs and SIDs are misunderstood by many instrument pilots when quizzed during instrument competency checks and flight tests. An IDP is designed solely for obstacle avoidance and is FAA's guarantee you won't hit anything during climb-out if the procedure is properly executed. While it isn't mandatory that you follow the IDP, the AIM makes it clear you must decide how to depart safely until radar service is provided by ATC.

IDPs are listed under Take-Off Minimums in the front of NOS chart books. Jepp chart users will find an IDP listed on the same page as the airport diagram.

A SID, on the other hand, is designed primarily to simplify clearance delivery procedures and also incorporates obstacle avoidance. Both NOS and Jeppesen include SIDs with the approach charts.

Airspace Concerns
If you follow the IDP for Brown Field to the letter, you'll eventually enter the San Diego TCA. This isn't a problem if you're already on an IFR clearance. But the Hawker pilot wanted to depart VFR and pick up his clearance after getting airborne, thereby avoiding a phone call to flight service to get a clearance with a void time. After reviewing the IDP for Brown Field, the pilot was concerned that, once airborne, he might not get his clearance soon enough and would risk a TCA bust.

Assure a Safe Climb
There's another AIM paragraph pertinent to this discussion. It says,

• Any aircraft departing VFR, either intending to or needing to obtain an IFR clearance en route, must be able to climb in VFR conditions to the MEA/MIA/MVA in order to receive the IFR clearance. The pilot will also be responsible for terrain/obstacle clearance until reaching the MEA/MIA/MVA. Any aircraft that cannot climb in VFR conditions to the MEA/MIA/MVA for IFR clearance, and accept responsibility for terrain/obstacle clearance should remain VFR; if unable, the pilot should advise the controller that an emergency is being declared.

In other words, if you want to depart VFR and pick up your clearance in the air, make sure you can climb to a safe altitude to do it. There's a reason the IDP for Brown Field takes you north and west when departing: the mountainous terrain to the east. The plan view of the Brown Field chart shows terrain at 3566 feet east of the field. The minimum safe altitude (MSA), which is based on PGY Vortac, is 7600 feet northeast of the vortac and 5000 feet southeast of the vortac.

VFR Chart Also Helpful
In addition, the San Diego VFR Terminal Area Chart shows a grid elevation of 4100 feet for the area east of Brown Field. During the investigation, NTSB asked the owner of the Hawker if he supplied the pilot with visual charts. The owner replied: "This is a ***damned jet outfit, we don't carry VFR charts."

The tragic part of this accident is a review of any chart would've told the pilot that a northeast departure at 3000 feet wasn't safe. During their final conversation, a gentle reminder by the briefer about the mountains would've been appropriate, but that wasn't his responsibility.

You'll recall the briefer commented to the pilot, "You are going out VFR. I keep forgetting that." This translates to: "You're departing VFR, so how you depart is up to you. It's your responsibility to do it safely."

When You Least Expect It

After takeoff, the proverbial last straw came when the pilot called for his clearance. He probably expected to get an immediate altitude and heading assignment, but was told instead to stand by since his clearance was no longer in the computer. Murphy's Law strikes again: If something can go wrong, it will and always when you least expect it.If you're superstitious and believe that bad luck comes in threes, this accident is a good example. The combination of a night departure, mountainous terrain and a close-by TCA warranted a fail-safe plan. In this case, getting the clearance on the ground would've resolved the problem. Sure, it would've meant calling by phone and getting a void time, which would've delayed the takeoff by several minutes; a small price to pay for the assurance of not hitting a mountain or busting a TCA.

Finally, there's nothing wrong with consulting FSS briefers, controllers and other pilots when flight planning from an unfamiliar airport. But you're the one that must ultimately be satisfied and comfortable with conducting the flight safely.

Confusing Instructions

*A*TC had a definite role in this one, but it's anciliary. In this case the controller departed from the cut-and-dried, rote phraseology and procedures that fill the controller's handbook.

The result was a series of confusing instructions, but that's not why the airplane hit the ground. The pilot failed to recognize that he was too low for an amazingly simple reason...read on.

Look Out Below!

Do you recall the last time you flew a picture-perfect instrument approach...one in which everything went according to Hoyle, including the controller's plans as well as yours? Depending on the scope of your IFR experience, that infrequent occasion may still be in store for you.

From at least one standpoint, flying an instrument approach has a lot in common with a golf swing; there are a whole bunch of things that can go wrong. For example, the weather might not be as good as forecast, or the winds are remarkably different from what you expected, or the destination VOR goes off the air just before you start the approach. And you thought that all you had to do was keep your eye on the ball!

Perhaps more important than realizing that actual IFR operations are not often textbook quality, you must be aware of the subtle effects on your performance when a flight starts going down the tubes. As we have seen over and over again in these recountings of aviation mishaps, an accident is the final event in a series, any one of which if altered, could have prevented the end result.

When a pilot recognizes that things are going sour, there are endless options; go somewhere else, ask for a different approach, maybe just be more sensitive to the situation. For reasons known only to those involved, the warning flags are not always heeded or not always in time to stop an accident sequence.

The private pilot in this case was not a beginner. He had 1500 hours of pilot time and had flown 30 hours in his single-engine retractable in the previous 90 days (which included 10 hours at night, eight hours of actual IFR and three hours of simulated instrument time). His second class medical certificate was only six months old and listed a routine limitation; he was required to wear eyeglasses whenever he acted as pilot in command.

The accident flight was the return from a golfing weekend in South Carolina, intending to land at the Robert J. Miller Airport in Tom's River, New Jersey. We don't have details of the conversations, but the record shows that the pilot received two weather briefings; one at 10:40 am and another just before departure at 5:40 pm.

A severe thunderstorm watch for eastern North Carolina and south-western Virginia was in effect that afternoon, but it didn't play a part in this accident. The culprit turned out to be much more benign weather. No alternate was listed on the IFR flight plan and we will assume that one was not required at the time the pilot was briefed.

Simple Approach

The instrument approach for Tom's River Airport is a straightforward localizer procedure, with a 500-foot MDA that places the airplane 418 feet above the runway. The final approach segment at the time of this accident was relatively short (2.8 miles), the altitude at the final approach fix was only 1000 feet msl, and the required visibility for straight-in category A and B operations was three-quarters of a mile. There's a simple transition from Coyle VOR, with sufficient time to get aligned and stabilized on the localizer.

The approach light system and the runway lights can be activated on the unicom frequency. There are no obstructions to complicate the approach. That part of New Jersey is as flat as your dining room table.

The airplane was totaled in this accident, but the pilot and two passengers survived. For this reason, we'll omit the airplane type and use a fictitious N number. The rest of the story is factual and is from the National Transportation Safety Board report.

We join the recorded communications as N1234A checks in with New York Center about 110 miles southwest of Tom's River.

N34A: New York Center, One-Two-Three-Four-Alpha, level seven thousand.
Center: Three-Four-Alpha, New York Center, radar contact. The Atlantic City altimeter is two-niner-six-niner.

(No acknowledgment from N34A and the world continued to turn despite the lack of a response, but controllers derive a lot of comfort from knowing that you've received that kind of information. If nothing else, it's a good idea to repeat the altimeter setting, which is often critical to instrument operations.)
There were no transmissions to or from N34A for nine minutes, then:

Center: Three-Four-Alpha, turn right heading 080, radar vector for traffic and then to Coyle.
(Good for the controller! Any time you are given a vector, you should know its purpose in the event you lose communications, you'll know where to go.)
N34A: Three-Four-Alpha, 080.

Another seven minutes elapsed with no radio traffic of significance to this story, then:

Center: Three-Four-Alpha, traffic at nine-thirty to ten o'clock, three miles, westbound at eight thousand.
N34A: Roger, tally ho.

(Many of you may cringe at the use of that Royal Air Force fighter-pilot expression, but you must admit that it gets the message across loud and clear with a minimum of verbiage. I doubt there's a controller around that doesn't know what that means. Also, we know that N34A is flying in reasonably clear air.)
In the next seven minutes, N34A and Center had nothing to say to each other, but the controllers were talking among themselves and N34A was handed off to McGuire Approach Control. (The flight was about to enter the airspace controlled by McGuire Air Force Base, 17 miles northwest of Tom's River.)

Center: Three-Four-Alpha, proceed direct Coyle and contact McGuire Approach on 127.5.
N34A: Three-Four-Alpha.

(Not all bad, but again, you'll do yourself and the controller a favor by repeating at least the numbers, e.g., two seven point five, just in case you misunderstood. It might save three or four additional communications.)

The pilot apparently got the correct frequency and a few seconds later:

N34A: McGuire, Three-Four-Alpha.
(It also helps to mention your altitude when checking in with a new controller. Your position and call sign are unmistakably clear on the radar screen, but everybody breathes easier when you confirm your altitude.)
McGuire: Three-Four-Alpha, McGuire, expect the localizer runway six approach at Robert J. Miller. The McGuire weather, sky partially obscured, measured ceiling 300 overcast, visibility one and one-half with fog. The wind is 070 at nine, altimeter 29.72. Our ceiling is two hundred variable to four hundred, fog is obscuring six tenths of the sky, and uh, the tower visibility here at McGuire is one-half mile with fog. You can expect lower in ten miles.
N34A: Roger.

Roger? Just plain roger, with no comment, no question, nothing? Either the pilot was fully expecting weather like this, or the near-minimums report didn't register. If nothing else, a resident and frequent flyer in that part of the country should be aware of the probability of dense fog on a spring evening when the wind blows off the ocean, only a few miles east of the airport. The preflight briefing surely mentioned these conditions.

What if the almost-certain missed approach were followed by a Murphy's Law communications failure? Remember that no alternate was filed and a no-radio situation (remote, to be sure, but possible) would leave the pilot, the controllers, the entire system in a bad way.

No Alternate Planned

The controller had the picture, however, and made the obvious suggestion very diplomatically:

McGuire: Three-Four-Alpha, in the event of a missed approach, what will your intentions be?

The pilot of N34A was not prepared for this; instead of a concise statement of his Plan B, he stammered:

N34A: Roger, uh, what's the, uh, Atlantic City, uh, weather?
McGuire: Okay, the last Atlantic City weather I had was, uh, 100 overcast and, uh, I didn't...I'll have to get you the visibility.
N34A: Check that, will you?

It's just as likely as not that this pilot was busy with the chores of flying the airplane and didn't take the time to listen to ATIS broadcasts, or call a flight service station to obtain current observations at nearby terminals. His apparent surprise on receiving the McGuire weather and lack of knowledge of conditions elsewhere suggests a lack of preparation.

At any rate, the McGuire controller was back on the air in less than one minute.

McGuire: Okay, uh, Three-Four-Alpha, the latest Atlantic City weather that we got was sky partially obscured, estimated ceiling was 400 overcast, with one and one-half in fog. The Lakehurst weather, sky obscured, measured ceiling 100 overcast, one and one-half miles in light drizzle and fog, three tenths of the sky obscured by fog.
N34A: Okay, uh, if we have to make a missed approach into Robert J. Miller, what we'd like to do then is, uh, go into Atlantic City, uh, Nafec.
McGuire: Okay.

N34A was heading toward an approach which promised little chance of success. The easterly wind continued to pump moisture from the ocean over the flat New Jersey terrain. The temperature was bound to drop somewhat as afternoon turned into evening and the fog that was already lowering visibility would only get worse.

The weather surprise was the first major discontinuity in an otherwise routine instrument flight. Should the pilot have immediately changed his plan and requested clearance for another terminal, one with a full ILS? That certainly seems reasonable, but remember that FAR Part 91 operators are permitted to take a look. (This is probably the most liberal, hazard-ridden rule in the book.)

There's nothing that says you can't sneak a peek, but in a situation like this, you can stack the odds more in your favor. An approach to minimums with knowledge that you probably won't break out sets the stage for stress, anxiety and the urge to press on, perhaps a few feet below MDA.

Two minutes pass, then:

McGuire: Three-Four-Alpha, descend and maintain two thousand.
N34A: Three-Four-Alpha leaving seven for two.

McGuire: And Three-Four-Alpha, what is your heading now?
N34A: Still heading of, uh, 030.
(Remember, he had previously been cleared direct to Coyle.)
McGuire: Okay, fly your present heading of 030 to intercept the, uh, Robert J. Miller localizer, report established.
N34A: Affirmative.

So far, a routine approach situation. Vectors to intercept a localizer course, descending to the minimum altitude for the initial segment of the approach. With no navigational chores except to maintain the assigned heading, the pilot had plenty of time to study the approach chart, set up his radios and review the missed approach procedure.

N34A was now close to the localizer and the controller observed that the altitude-to-lose was going to conflict with the distance-to-go.

McGuire: Three-Four-Alpha, turn left heading of, uh, 010, vectors for descent. That'll give you a little bit more time to get down there.
N34A: Descending.

Confusing Intercept

McGuire: I'll give you a turn in the back from the left side of the localizer intercept.
N34A: Okay, in other words, the localizer will be coming in on my left?
McGuire: You'll be coming in to the localizer from the left, localizer will be on your right.
N34A: Understand.
(It gets worse.)
McGuire: Unless you think you can make the descent, uh, on the 030 heading to join, but I show you out of 6200. What are you doing, a thousand feet a minute now?
N34A: About seven hundred feet a minute.
McGuire: Roger, just fly a ten heading, I'll bring you in from the, uh, the north side.
N34A: Thank you, guy.

If ever there was a situation in which a controller had too much to say, offered too much help, you've just read about it.

Not only were the instructions about the localizer intercept confusing, the question about the rate of descent may well have introduced a sense of urgency and may have snookered the pilot into increasing his vertical speed. Yet another nonstandard event in what was beginning to look like one of those dangerous series.

Controllers can't fly our airplanes, but they can make subtle inputs which are difficult to ignore. As you'll see, rate of descent played a major role in the outcome.

Ten minutes, four heading changes and several thousand feet later, N34A was eastbound on a vector to intercept the localizer (from the north side), and was instructed to report established on the final approach course.

McGuire: Three-Four-Alpha, are you on the localizer now?
N34A: Yes, coming up on it now, sir.
McGuire: All right sir, your position is, uh, eight and one-half miles southwest of R.J. Miller, you're cleared straight-in localizer approach runway six, report cancellation of IFR in the air or on the ground via the, uh, phone, uh, in the back of the building after landing.
N34A: Roger.

At this point in a textbook approach, N34A should have been established on the localizer at 1900 feet msl, airspeed at or near that to be used for the final segment, elevator forces trimmed, which is what a stabilized approach is all about. Some pilots prefer to have the landing gear down here, anticipating only a slight power reduction to start the airplane downhill at the final approach fix. Other would wait until the FAF to lower the gear, depending on the drag to commence the descent.

Either way, a descent rate of only 500 feet per minute would put the airplane at MDA well before reaching the airport, with plenty of time to make the land/missed approach decision.

But the pilot of N34A didn't afford himself that luxury. One minute and ten seconds after N34A acknowledged the approach clearance:

McGuire: Three-Four-Alpha, the McGuire altimeter 29.72. Check your altitude sir, I show you at 300 feet.
Unknown: (Sound of mike being keyed.)
McGuire: Three-Four-Alpha, radar contact is lost five miles southwest of R.J. Miller Airport.

N34A plowed into the trees and crashed less than a mile inside the Soite Intersection. If the published altitude (1900 feet) had in fact been maintained until that point, the required descent rate to impact would have been 2700 fpm. While the aircraft was capable of that, it doesn't make sense at this point during any instrument approach.

A more likely scenario would have the pilot commencing the descent at some earlier point, or perhaps continuing the rapid descent unwittingly urged by the controller earlier. The result seems to point to one of two conditions; either N34A fell out of the sky at an alarming rate, or it continued a normal descent with the pilot paying no attention to his altitude.

The series of events philosophy was certainly evident in this accident sequence. The pilot was apparently surprised by weather conditions and was determined to attempt the procedure in the face of almost certain missed approach conditions. He was undecided about an alternative course of action, had some confusing vectors and instructions and an invitation to use a high rate of descent. Any one of these would have justified a decision to break it off and go somewhere else, or at least fly a wide pattern to give the pilot time to think things through. Landing at some other airport would have been preferable to landing in the trees.

What's Your Tolerance?

Each of us has a threshold of tolerance for unusual instructions and procedures, and that threshold can only be determined by experience. Even if you put yourself in a good simulator and find out how much you can take, be prepared to alter that perception in the real world, as each situation is subtly different than the controlled atmosphere of simulation or instructional flight.

When nonstandard events stack up, the smart pilot recognizes the situation and takes steps to manage the additional risk that has presented itself. Perhaps the most common situation is one in which a pilot allows himself to be rushed through an approach. There's nothing wrong with hurrying, but there's a lot wrong with being hurried. (The hurrier I go, the behinder I get?)

Pilot Insight

If you are still wondering why this accident occurred, the answer is astoundingly simple. It was provided by the pilot, who was interviewed by accident investigators shortly after the crash: The pilot told us that there was nothing wrong with the aircraft. The problem was that his bifocals prevented him from seeing all of the instrument panel without bending his neck and looking upward. He had to bend his neck upward in order to see the altimeter. For some reason, he did not look at the altimeter. The approach controller warned him of his altitude and it was right after the warning that he hit the trees.

'Nuff said.

• Section Three •

Equipment Failures

Surviving Without Gyros

T hink of your scan. What's in the middle of it? Right—the attitude indicator. The AI is so central to instrument flight that losing it can all too easily cause a pilot to rapidly start spiraling out of control. There aren't many pieces of equipment so vital to survival in IMC.

We're supposed to be able to fly competently on partial panel, but many of us aren't all that good at it. Here's the story of one pilot who found the loss of his AI too much to handle.

Three Minus Two Equals One

Would you like to fly IFR with a virtual guarantee that you'd always have a working attitude indicator? To accomplish this, all you have to do is modify your airplane to comply with FAR 121.305. It would take a lot of money and it might be difficult to find room for all the gear, but here's what you'd have: two ordinary attitude indicators, plus a third one that's self-powered. The self-powered AI works for at least 30 minutes after a total failure of the electrical system, operates independently of the other two AIs and comes on line automatically when the power fails.

For many single-engine airplanes, this modification would cost more than the airplane is worth. It's another example of regulatory overkill that forces air carriers to take seemingly extreme steps to ensure the highest standard of care in flight operations.

No-Gyro Land

If your flight instruments are powered by either air pressure or vacuum, and the pump fails in flight, you might suddenly be in no-gyro land. Well, it isn't quite that drastic, since the usual installation consists of an air-driven AI and HI, with an electric turn coordinator. The electric gyro is a safety net of sorts, but it only works if you know what you're doing.

When you start with three gyro instruments and lose two, you should be able to get home on the one that remains. If you aren't able to fly needle, ball and airspeed, you've fallen below the minimum standards of pilot proficiency and three minus two can equal zero. Here's what happened to one pilot who fell into this category.

Return Flight

This 20-year old aviator had almost 1100 hours and a pocketful of credentials: commercial, multi-engine and CFI. He was at work when the accident occurred, returning to Poughkeepsie, NY after dropping off a passenger at Cape Cod, MA. The pilot of Piper Dakota N2186B checked in with Boston Center shortly after leveling at 6000 feet and two minutes later:

N86B: Boston, it's Eight-Six-Bravo.
Center: Eight-Six-Bravo, go ahead.
N86B: Yes sir, I just got a light on the vacuum pump and we're low on suction here. Any chance of direct Kingston [VOR]?
Center: Okay sir, you'd probably have to make the instrument approach. Let me take a look at the weather. Hang on.

It was dark by now and there was weather. The Dakota was IMC and, to his credit, the controller came up with a good suggestion:

Center: Two-One-Eight-Six-Bravo, I think it might be quicker if you go over Pawling [VOR] and make the straight-in VOR/DME, rather than go to Kingston and then fly the procedure turn. What do you think?
N86B: That sounds good to me. If I could get direct Pawling now, I'd appreciate it.
Center: (After a conversation with approach control) Two-One-Eight-Six-Bravo, you're cleared direct Pawling, expect no delay. Plan on the VOR/DME to Runway 24.
N86B: Okay, thanks a lot, I appreciate it. And Boston, just to let you know, Eight-Six-Bravo is no-gyros at this time.
Center: Eight-Six-Bravo, no gyros, okay, thank you.

In the next few minutes, the controller gave the pilot a radar fix, advised him to expect descent in three to four miles and passed along a pirep of layered clouds down to 2500 feet. At this time, the Dakota was about 18 miles and eight minutes from the VOR. It was going to be a long eight minutes.

Everybody Gets It

There are two things that happen when a pilot finds him/herself operating partial panel: first, some disorientation will occur no matter how experienced the aviator might be and, second, the time from loss or normal visual clues (the AI) to the onset of disorientation will vary greatly among pilots.

Before you old-timers get upset with the first condition, consider this: Human beings aren't equipped to maintain spatial orientation when visual clues are lost, hence all of us suffer some confusion about which end is up. Pilots trained to overcome the resultant illusions by referring to the remaining instruments and who can operate the controls properly in this situation are the ones who can continue flying. Pilots who fall prey to the illusions and/or are unable to maintain control with only needle, ball and airspeed are destined for big trouble. It's usually the final episode in their lives.

Things gone awry

When the pilot of N86B acknowledged the radar fix and the weather report, he added, So far, it doesn't seem to be too much of a problem. This was no doubt a reference to his ability to keep the shiny side up without the AI and HI. But one minute later, the controller noticed a deviation:

Center: Two-One-Eight-Six-Bravo, I show you turning, ah, what's your...disregard, my radar showed a bad hit on you. It looked like you were turning southbound. Disregard, I show you tracking towards Pawling again.
N86B: For a second I had it in a turn. Right now I'm back on course.
Center: Two-One-Eight-Six-Bravo, are your gyros affecting your navigation to Pawling? If so, I can probably give you no-gyro vectors to the radial to intercept.
N86B: If you can give me a vector, I'd appreciate that.
Center: Okay, are you in a right turn right now? It's hard to tell.
N86B: Well, let's see how I can deal [with it] on my own here a little bit and if gets to be too much of a problem, we'll see what we can work out.
Center: Okay, it looks to me like you just made a three-sixty right there.
N86B: Okay.

Let's freeze the problem for a moment and consider what might be happening to this pilot. Disorientation had obviously entered the picture, otherwise N86B would have continued with no change in heading. The controller's comment about a bad radar hit and an apparent turn could have fertilized the seeds of confusion that had already been sown in the pilot's mind.

From Direct to Indirect

Here's where strict discipline is needed. Think back to the last time you flew into a cloud. Remember the adjustment you had to make when you started flying on the gauges, the way you had to bear down on the basics and force yourself to cross-check, interpret and control? Do you remember how uncomfortable it was for a short time as you acclimated to the change? The same shift in emphasis must take place when your world turns to partial panel.

Now, instead of direct indications of attitude and heading, everything is indirect. Airspeed, altimeter and vertical speed tell you about pitch, the turn coordinator and magnetic compass are your only indications of bank. Going from direct to indirect is a huge change. It isn't going to happen automatically or instantaneously...you've got to make a huge adjustment.

No Gyro Vectors

Back to N86B. Twenty seconds after the last communication, the controller must have seen another deviation on his display.

Center: Eight-Six-Bravo, why don't you stop your turn right where you are now and we'll see how it looks.
N86B: Okay, sir.

Thirty seconds go by, then:

Center: Two-One-Eight-Six-Bravo, turn right.
N86B: Eight-Six-Bravo, turn right.
Center: And Eight-Six-Bravo, this will be no-gyro vectors.
N86B: Thank you.

Strange things happen in our heads (all our heads, no one is exempt) when we're deprived of visual clues or presented with conflicting information. A turn might feel like no turn at all and vice versa. A climb or descent might feel like a turn and vice versa. There are some solid legs you can stand on.

Don't Change Anything

If your airplane was properly trimmed for level flight when you discovered the gyros weren't working, it should continue in level flight if you keep your hands off the controls and change neither power nor trim. Also consider if the turn needle is standing straight up or the miniature airplane is wings level and the ball is centered, the airplane isn't turning. Your primary job becomes one of managing these conditions and it isn't as difficult as it seems.

Don't Rush

You shouldn't be in a hurry to descend (you can let down slowly when it's necessary), so don't change power, pitch or trim. Leave well enough alone and that includes taking your hands off the controls and letting the airplane fly itself. When you must descend, squeeze off one inch of manifold pressure or 100 rpm and see what results. Then throttle back one inch or 100 rpm at a time if a more rapid descent is required.

Airspeed will stay within 5-10 knots of the trim speed throughout the descent and level-off if you handle the throttle smoothly and slowly. When you must slow down, back off a bit on the throttle, squeeze in a bit of nose-up trim (enough to hold altitude) and keep it up until the desired airspeed is reached. Of course, you need to apply and hold whatever rudder pressure is needed to keep the ball centered.

Stopping the Turn

So much for the level part; how about straight? Remember, if the turn needle is standing straight up or the wings are level and the ball is centered, the airplane isn't turning. If you can keep the needle and ball centered, there won't be a heading change. Your inner ear and the seat of your pants might be shouting Turn! Turn! Turn! but if those two conditions are met, there is no turn.

Especially during the first few minutes of a partial panel episode, this should be a mechanical, robotic operation. When the turn needle moves from center or the wings move, apply aileron to keep it straight or level. When the ball drifts right or left, step on it and apply rudder pressure on the same side the ball is displaced. After a while, this combination becomes a lot smoother. It's nothing more than maintaining coordinated flight. This is the part most pilots don't seem to understand: getting into the partial panel groove takes a while. You can't expect it to happen right away.

A Few No-Gyro Turns

After a minute and a half and a couple of no-gyro turns, the controller had the Dakota lined up for the approach.

Center: Two-One-Eight-Six-Bravo, your present heading looks pretty good. You can plan on intercepting the Kingston Zero-Six-Two radial and commencing the VOR/DME approach straight-in once you intercept.
N86B: Okay.
Center: Two-One-Eight-Six-Bravo, descend and maintain 5000.
N86B: Descend to 5000 now, Eight-Six-Bravo.

The pilot might have been staggering on the brink of complete disorientation, needing only a nudge to push him over. A pitch change to start the descent might have been the catalyst, but whatever the reason, his acknowledgment of the lower altitude was his last transmission. The radar plot showed a three-sixty in 74 seconds, followed by a one-eighty to the right and a 90-degree turn to the left. The altitude varied between 5700 and 6300 feet before radar contact was lost. The wreckage was scattered over a half-mile of countryside, strongly suggestive of an in-flight break-up.

The odds of a simultaneous or immediate failure of both vacuum pump and electrical system are astronomical and, if that happens, there's precious little you can do. But light airplanes can be flown quite well with needle, ball and airspeed, if you know how to do it. We all had to demonstrate at least minimum proficiency on partial panel at one time, but most pilots seldom refresh their skills. If your answer to the question, "When was the last time you flew all the way through an instrument approach without gyros?" leaves you a little shaky about how you'd handle an actual occurrence, best hire a good CFII and retrain.

A constant risk

Boaters carry life jackets to ensure their survivability in case the old tub springs a leak. It probably won't happen, but what if it does? Following the same reasoning, pilots should be proficient in partial panel. Gyro failure is just one of the risks we assume every time we fly IFR.

Vacuum Failure: Nail in the Coffin

T his accident is as much about judgment, weather, hypoxia and spatial disorientation as it is about equipment failure. But a vacuum failure played a very important role in it.

The accident is a classic case: There were multiple causes, any one of which may not have proved to be a serious problem, but together they proved fatal.

Four Links in a Chain

The Appalachian mountains top out at 6600 feet. While this might not seem very high for VFR flight, the minimum en route altitude (MEA) required over these mountains for IFR flight can result in hypoxia if the pilot doesn't use supplemental oxygen. Hypoxia was the first link in a chain of events that led to this month's accident.

The pilot in this case received a preflight briefing that revealed a cold front from northeast to southwest across his intended route from Atlanta to central Ohio. It was December and, as you might expect, moderate to severe rime icing was forecast between 2000 and 18,000 feet, along with moderate to locally severe turbulence below 5000 feet.

This was a well-defined cold front. Stations on either side of the front were reporting VFR conditions, while in the vicinity of the front, ceilings were from 2500 to 6500 overcast with good visibility. The freezing level was 9000 feet.

Decision Time

Cloud bases were too low for comfortable VFR flight over the mountains. The MEA required at least 9000 feet early in the flight. The pilot, who was flying a Cessna Turbo 210, asked the briefer about cloud tops and explained that his airplane had de-icing equipment, but that he'd prefer to be on top if possible. The briefer told him of a pirep over Knoxville (approximately mid-route) that indicated tops at 11,500 feet and clear above.

Flight Watch Update

The airplane departed the Atlanta area at 8:49 a.m. and was cleared to 11,000 feet. At 9:14, the pilot called Atlanta Flight Watch for a weather update, which confirmed the forecast conditions at his destination. The pilot gave a pirep, "...tops of the clouds ten point five all quadrants, back towards Atlanta."

At that time, he was 43 miles north of Atlanta. The FSS specialist said:

FSS: You might want to double check, as you continue northbound, might have a potential icing problem.
Pilot: Roger, we have de-icing equipment, but right now we're looking good.

The Cessna was in clear air at 11,000 feet, after climbing through the freezing level without incident. The Cessna Turbo 210 was one of the first single-engine airplanes to be certificated for flight into known icing. If there was any ice during the climb out of Atlanta, the equipment worked properly.

Cloud tops associated with a cold front usually aren't flat. In this case, there were two factors that caused the tops to rise: the slope of the frontal surface as it bulled its way southeastward and the mechanical lifting as the air mass crossed the mountains.

Radio communications at 9:57 indicated that the tops were close to the Cessna's altitude:

Pilot: Atlanta, Four-Six-Charlie, we'd like to go up to eleven thousand.
Center: Ah, I show you level at one-one thousand.
Pilot: I'm sorry, I'd like to go up to twelve thousand.
Center: Roger, Four-Six-Charlie, climb and maintain one-two thousand.

Creeping Hypoxia?

Pilots sometimes make mistakes like that as a result of inattention or some other state of mind. This appeared to be more than a slip of the tongue. It raises the possibility that the pilot began to suffer hypoxia. Investigators did not find any evidence that oxygen was used during the flight. This was link number two in the chain of events.

There's nothing illegal about flying without oxygen at 11,000 feet, but all of us are affected to some degree when flying above ten grand. This pilot may have been affected by anxiety due to an impending encounter with higher, ice-filled clouds. Two minutes later, he called Atlanta Flight Watch for more information:

Pilot: Roger Atlanta, Centurion Four-Six-Charlie, 42 DME north of Knoxville, request the current weather at London, Kentucky and also Knoxville.
FSS: Okay Four-Six-Charlie, Knoxville has an estimated ceiling of 6000 broken, visibility unlimited. London reports estimated ceiling of 2800 broken, 8000 overcast, visibility 12, temperature 53, dew point 47, wind 240 degrees at 8, and the altimeter is 2998. Ah, London reported a thunderstorm ended 28 minutes past the hour, movement unknown. It looks like your tops up London way are about 12,000 feet.
Pilot: What's the freezing level around Knoxville?
FSS: Okay, the freezing level is at niner thousand.
Pilot: Roger, thank you. We're going to return to Knoxville.
FSS: Okay, Four-Six-Charlie, and are you on top or between layers?
Pilot: We're on top at twelve-five.

On top at 12,500 feet? Four-Six-Charlie was operating on an IFR clearance at 12,000 feet. It's unlikely that a pilot would fly 500 feet off his assigned altitude, much less tell anyone about it. Something isn't right here.

Bad to Worse

The problems began to snowball with the next series of communications. At 10:02 am, the pilot called Atlanta Center and asked for clearance to 13,000 feet. The controller answered, "Centurion Four-Six-Charlie, Atlanta," which implied that he didn't understand the request or needed to coordinate with another controller.

There was no communication from the Cessna for the next minute-and-a-half, then:

Pilot: Centurion Four-Eight-Four-Six- Charlie.
Center: Centurion Four-Six-Charlie, Atlanta
Pilot: Roger, Four-Six-Charlie has lost vacuum and I'd like an immediate clearance back to Knoxville.

There is link number three.
It's pretty clear that the pilot was struggling with an instrument

problem several minutes before he asked for a clearance to Knoxville. He probably wouldn't have asked for weather reports at London and Knoxville if he intended to continue to Ohio, unless something had gone wrong.

The recorded radar data showed that the Centurion climbed to 13,300 feet. Was the pilot attempting to stay above the clouds, which were growing as he approached the frontal zone, or was he in the clouds and having difficulty maintaining altitude without primary flight instruments?

The pilot's report of the vacuum failure and his use of the word "immediate" prompted the controller to consider the situation an emergency:

Center: Roger, Four-Six-Charlie, cleared direct Knoxville, descend and maintain 8000.
Pilot: Roger, we'll turn around for Knoxville, going down to eight. Thank you.

Between 10:04 and 10:06, there was no communication with N46C. The Atlanta Center controller coordinated the change of flight plan and the emergency status with Knoxville Approach Control. During this time, the airplane climbed to 13,600 feet, started a turn to the right and descended to 12,800 feet. The Cessna turned 270 degrees in 40 seconds, more than twice standard rate. A turn direct Knoxville required a heading change of only 135 degrees. Disorientation and loss of control were link number four.

The controller noticed that N46C wasn't descending and reminded the pilot.

Center: Four-Six-Charlie, you are cleared to continue your descent to maintain six thousand.
Pilot: Roger, we're still at twelve-five.
Center: Roger, your discretion, maintain six thousand.
Pilot: Going down to six.
Center: Four-Six-Charlie, are you requesting special handling into Knoxville?
Pilot: Negative, everything's okay except for the vacuum.

His last transmission was a lot on the hopeful side. The radar plots indicated that the airplane started a right turn. It turned 430 degrees, at five degrees per second, and descended to 6300 feet at a rate of 5000 feet per minute. Clearly, the pilot had lost control and his attempts at recovery caused the airplane to disintegrate.

Everything indicated that the pilot was conscientious, well-trained and experienced in his airplane. There was a progression of events, though, which brought the airplane down.

The Four Events

First, there was the combination of terrain and weather, which, if icing and turbulence were to be avoided, required the cruising altitude of 11,000 feet.

The second event was the pilot's failure to use supplemental oxygen. The effects of hypoxia vary among individuals. Our tolerance is dependent upon state of mind, physical condition and the events of the moment, to name a few. When affected by hypoxia, a pilot's response is abnormal.

When the vacuum pump failed (this was confirmed during the investigation), the third link in the chain was forged. At this point, the pilot made a good decision to proceed to an alternate. The choice of alternate and the method employed to get there leads you to believe that the pilot's mental processes were foggy.

Weather reports, backed up by spectacular satellite photographs, showed beautiful weather ahead of the front. The frontal zone was well defined, with North and South Carolina basking in sunshine and clear skies. The pilot must have been aware that there were VFR conditions a short distance behind him when the vacuum pump quit. For reasons that remain unknown, he fixed his attention on an immediate descent to Knoxville, the nearest large airport.

The fourth and final link in the chain of events was disorientation and loss of control. Perhaps he could have controlled the airplane and flown it out of trouble without gyroscopic instruments under less demanding circumstances, without the added problems of anxiety and hypoxia.

In retrospect, poor decision-making was the heart of this pilot's problems. When he observed higher clouds along the route, there were three reasonable options: Continue at the present altitude and turn around at the first sign of icing; turn back to avoid icing altogether; or put on an oxygen mask and climb. The clear air immediately behind the airplane represented the best escape route.

The pilot's failure to inquire about weather conditions elsewhere and his request for an immediate descent into Knoxville suggest that his thinking was not clear. If nothing else, a 180-degree turn and a return to clear air would have reduced the partial- panel operation to one simple turn and several minutes of straight and level flight. A landing at Knoxville entailed descending through five or six thousand feet of ice-laden clouds and possibly a partial-panel approach.

When a proposed flight will put you between a rock and a hard place with regard to terrain and top-of-the-weather, think twice about departing. Don't allow a lack of oxygen or limited airplane performance to put you into a situation that will compromise your ability to think clearly if something goes wrong. In any IFR situation, know which way is out and how far to safe weather.

Finally, when something goes wrong, keep your head on straight and remember the cardinal rule for success in aviation, *fly the airplane!* There is absolutely nothing more important to your survival than to keep your flying machine under control.

Electrical Failure

O kay, you lose your alternator, and you're flying on battery power alone. You've just left on an IFR flight plan, but the weather is still VFR—you haven't hit any IMC yet. What do you do?

Turn back, right?

What if you're on a schedule? What if you absolutely, positively have to make it to your destination and you really believe you can make on the battery? What now?

Most of us would turn back, but not all. This is the story of a commuter pilot who bet against the life of his battery and lost.

Trying to Beat the Clock

Years ago, there was a television game show called *Beat The Clock*, where contestants ran around and tried to complete a series of tasks in a predetermined amount of time. The winner was the person who could correctly complete all the tasks in the right order before time ran out. Those who couldn't complete the tasks on time went home with a consolation prize.

The two commuter pilots in this accident played a similar game when they flew a medium-size twin on battery power only, following a generator failure. Instead of taking action in time to ensure the safety of themselves and their passengers, they continued into deteriorating weather. Ten people died. The captain's determination to make it home undoubtedly clouded their decision making.

Behind Schedule

Air Illinois 710 (a Hawker Siddley 748) was a scheduled flight from

Chicago, IL to Carbondale, IL with an en route stop in Springfield, IL. Delayed getting out of Chicago, the flight landed in Springfield 45 minutes late. The crew then called flight service for the latest Carbondale weather, which was: 2000 overcast, visibility two miles in light rain and fog, temperature 65o and dew point 63°. Springfield was reporting 2800 broken, 4500 overcast, six miles in haze, temperature 65°, dew point 62°.

The flight departed Springfield at 6:20 p.m. for the 45-minute trip to Carbondale, the crew's home base. After contacting Springfield Departure, they were cleared to 5000 feet and direct to the Carbondale Vortac. We have the benefit of the crew's actions and conversations since the airplane was equipped with a cockpit voice recorder.

During climb out, the generator warning light came on. This airplane had a history of problems with the generator on the right engine. So when the warning light came on, the first officer assumed that the right generator had failed and punched the corresponding circuit breaker to take the generator off-line. Unfortunately, it was the left generator that quit.

Realizing his mistake, the first officer tried to get the right generator back on line, but wasn't successful. The airplane's electrical system was now operating on battery power alone. They had been airborne only a minute and a half. A turn back to the airport was in order to check out the problem while the weather was still VFR.

Instead, the crew told Springfield Departure they had a slight electrical problem and would keep ATC advised. The controller asked if they wanted to return to Springfield. The crew declined, instead asking to stay as low as possible. They were cleared to 3000 feet.

The first officer again tried unsuccessfully to get the right generator back on line. How frustrating, a perfectly good generator putting out current and they couldn't use it. The first officer told the captain that battery power was depleting rapidly.

Scud Running?

At 6:27 p.m., the flight was talking to Kansas City Center and the following conversation took place:

710: We are kinda having an unusual request here. We would like to go down to 2000 feet and if we have to go VFR, that's fine. But we'd like you to keep your eye on us if you can.
Center: Illinois Seven-Ten, I can't clear you down to 2000. I don't even think I can keep you on radar if I, if I had to if you went down that far.
710: All right, fine. Thank you.

Center: Did you copy that?
710: I'm sorry, I missed that.
Center: I won't be able to clear you down to 2000. It's below the lowest usable altitude I can give you. If you went down there VFR, I doubt I can keep you in radar.
710: Okay, fine. Thank you.

The crew turned off electrical equipment to reduce battery drain; nav lights, strobes, cabin lights and continued until they were operating with a single nav/com and the transponder. The first officer continued trying to get the working generator back on line, but to no avail.

Passengers Concerned

By this time, some passengers were asking the flight attendant why there weren't any cabin lights on. It was dark now and they were probably in IMC. The flight attendant asked the crew about the problem. "We have a little bit of an electrical problem here, but we're going to continue to Carbondale. We had to shut off all excess lights," replied the captain. The first officer stated that they would be in Carbondale by 7 p.m.

TRW in Area

As if the generator problem wasn't enough, there were scattered thunderstorms in the area. Other flights were talking to Center about deviating around weather. The first officer turned on the weather radar to evaluate the situation, but radar needs several minutes to warm up before use...and battery power was still depleting.

About two-thirds of the way to the Southern Illinois Airport (Carbondale), the crew pulled out the ILS Runway 18 approach chart for review. Then:

Captain: Is that lightning off your right side?
First Officer: Yeah.

Getting more anxious by the moment as he watched the battery power decrease on the volt meter, the first officer remarked:

First Officer: I don't know if we have enough juice to get out of this.
Captain: Squawk your radio failure.

Things were going down hill rapidly.
Seconds later, the Center controller announced, "I've lost radar

contact."

The crew didn't respond to this or any further calls. The battery power was probably so depleted at this point that the radios were useless.

Capt: Watch my altitude, I'm going down to 2400.
First Officer: We're losing everything. Down to about 13 volts.
Capt: Okay, watch my altitude.
First Officer: Okay, 2400.
Capt: Do you have any instruments?
First Officer: Say again?
Capt: Do you have any instruments, do you have a horizon?

That was the last comment before crashing into an open pasture. The airplane hit the ground in an eight-degree descending flight path and in a 33-degree right bank. The two pilots, flight attendant and seven passengers were killed.

Needless Tragedy

This accident should never have happened. There were several points during this brief flight when disaster could have been averted. The generator failed only moments after takeoff. Even though the ceiling was at 2800 feet, the crew could have made the proverbial one-eighty in VFR conditions and landed to check out the problem. Instead, they chose to press on.

At no point during the flight did either pilot ever discuss how long battery power would last. The first officer continuously monitored the volt meter, which indicated how fast the battery was being depleted, but there were no indications that he calculated the time remaining for current electrical load. The captain didn't seem too interested, since his response to the depleting power was to shut off more equipment, but neither did he calculate the time remaining.

This airplane was equipped with nicad batteries. During its investigation, the National Transportation Safety Board reviewed the battery manufacturer's handbook, which states, *The nicad battery's voltage remains relatively constant until very nearly all its capacity is discharged, at which point the voltage drops off sharply. And an electrical design engineer testified, You can't tell [battery] capacity by voltage.*

Calculating Power

In other words, the only way to estimate the time remaining on the battery is to calculate the total electrical load and divide that into the capacity of the battery. For example, a 60-amp hour battery will produce 60 amps of power for one hour, 30 amps for two hours, etc. After estimating the electrical load that was probably in use, NTSB calculated that the battery should have provided power for 30 minutes. The battery actually lasted 31 minutes before the avionics failed.

One or both of the pilots probably believed they could stretch the power for the 45-minute flight. But in this case, a miss was as good as a mile. They needed a fully-functioning electrical system to fly an instrument approach at their destination, where the weather was 2000 overcast, 1-1/2 miles in light rain and fog.

Excessive Risk-Taking?

The captain's continued request for a lower altitude suggests that he believed they could sneak under the cloud bases and continue VFR. NTSB interviewed other Air Illinois pilots, who described the captain as a company man and always in a hurry to make schedules. Apparently, the captain was so determined to make his schedules that he would fly close to or under thunderstorms to avoid delays and would over-speed the airplane during descents to save time.

Ahead of the Airplane?

The first officer was described by the other pilots as very knowledgeable and always ahead of the airplane. In this case though, he made a dangerous assumption. Instead of confirming the failed generator, he assumed that the right generator had failed due to previous problems.

Always take time and confirm the failed component in an emergency. Jumping to conclusions causes pilots to misidentify a failed engine...or generator. You're probably familiar with the saying about the word assume, it makes an ass out of u and me.

Opportunities Missed

Another tragic aspect to this story concerns the missed opportunities for this flight to have landed safely. The airplane ground track shows that the crew passed six airports to which they could have diverted. One of those airports was Scott Air Force Base, where precision approach radar was available.

Know Your Airplane

Do you know how long your aircraft battery would last if the alternator/generator quit? Listed below is the power used by the equipment on a typical general aviation airplane:

- ADF .... 5 amps
- Audio panel .... 5 amps
- Cabin lights .... 5 amps
- Com/nav .... 5 amps
- DME .... 5 amps
- Engine gauges .... 5 amps
- Flaps .... 8 amps
- Landing gear .... 5 amps
- Pitot heat .... 10 amps
- Strobes .... 15 amps
- Transponder .... 5 amps

Let's assume that your airplane has a 35-amp hour battery. This means that the battery will produce 35 amps for one hour or one amp for 35 hours. Using the above list, you could run the ADF, audio panel, one com/nav, engine gauges, pitot heat and transponder for one hour. This assumes that the battery is in good condition and that you detect the alternator/generator failure as soon as it occurs.

The pitot heat is the biggest draw on the system. If you can get by without it, your time is considerably extended. Even if you know that you can last more than an hour, plan to be on the ground in half the time. Set a limit and stick to it at all costs. Don't let the nearness of home tempt you into stretching it.Just as with low fuel, this is another situation where you should not play Beat The Clock. Losing at this game means you might not get to go home.

Reacting
Appropriately

C risis. Your gyro has failed, and you're in the soup. Not only that, you're in a Cessna 152, a decidedly marginal airplane when it comes to flying IFR. If you're like most of us, this will result in a big shot of adrenaline pumping into your system. Some people will freeze, others will panic and react inappropriately. Some will handle the emergency well (usually, those that have practiced it).

A gyro failure in IMC is not a trivial event. But it need not be disastrous if the PIC keeps a clear head and takes the best course of action.

This accident concerns a flight instructor who, rather than considering all his options, fixated instead on trying to reach VFR. As we'll see, this proved to be his undoing. What is most surprising about this accident is that not only was the instructor a CFII, the gyro that failed wasn't even the "important" one. It was the heading indicator.

Decisions, Decisions

You've probably been taught that when push comes to shove, you can put a light airplane in the tops of trees and probably escape with minor injuries. This takes into account an impact at the slowest possible speed, which in a Cessna 152, could be as low as 30-35 knots. Try this at cruise speed, though, and you should expect the worst, as was the case in this accident.

Accident Scene

The accident scene from the ground was an awesome confirmation of the kinetic energy developed by a Cessna 152 moving at 100-120 knots.

The NTSB report indicated that, *The wreckage distribution path ex-*

tended more than 600 feet through the densely wooded area. Initial impact occurred in the top of a more than 80-foot tall pine tree. Major portions of the right wing separated from the aircraft during the initial sequence. After a 200-foot length it settled back into the tops of oaks and pines.

Principal impact occurred approximately 50 feet above the ground in an 18-inch diameter pine. A four-foot long log was carried to the ground by the wreckage. The engine separated from the airframe with the firewall and instrument panel still attached and came to rest 75 feet beyond the central wreckage area.

Needless to say, the two occupants didn't survive. But there was sufficient evidence to trace the decisions that led to this accident. Life as a pilot seems to be comprised of one decision after another, and as usual, a break anywhere in the chain of events would have produced a favorable outcome to this accident.

IFR to VFR Departure

The flight was part of a state technical school flight program in Ruston, Louisiana. The Ruston Airport was IFR that morning and the instrument portion of the flight was planned only to get to VFR conditions so the student could proceed with his cross-country work.

A cold front was moving across northern Louisiana, with low ceilings and visibilities in the vicinity of the front, but with good weather behind it. Dallas and Shreveport were in fine shape and forecast to stay that way all day. El Dorado, Arkansas (40 miles north of Ruston) was also VFR under the influence of a high pressure system behind the front.

The supervisor of flying briefed the flight instructor to head for El Dorado if any problems were encountered.

To understand the weather conditions in the area, consider the statement of a commuter pilot who had flown from Monroe to Ruston just before the C-152 departed: "I can remember looking down and commenting to my copilot that the weather around Ruston seemed lower than at Monroe and that it didn't look like very good VFR conditions. I would estimate about 1000 scattered to broken and two miles visibility."

In addition, consider that two hunters within a half-mile of the accident site heard the impact, but didn't see the airplane in the rain because the clouds were at treetop level.

Gyro Failure

The Cessna departed Ruston at 12:30 p.m. and was cleared on course to maintain 4000 feet. Eight minutes into the flight, and very shortly after leveling at 4000, the flight instructor said to Fort Worth Center: "This is 527, we need a descent out of the clouds. We've just lost our gyros. We want to return to Ruston."

Time for a decision. In weather, in an airplane with minimal IFR equipment, the instrument failure required that something be done to solve the problem. Continuing to Houston (the original destination) was not a good choice. That would entail flying along, if not through, the frontal weather.

A return to the departure airport was not a bad choice, although the weather was moving toward Ruston. How about El Dorado, a solid-gold alternate only 40 miles away and the safe haven briefed by the supervisor before takeoff?

Get Back to VFR

The CFI apparently decided to go back. The controller didn't get the message the first time:

ATC: Cessna 527, you say you lost your gyro?
527: Affirmative. I would like to descend through the clouds and go back to Ruston. See if we could descend, get back to VFR.

The transmission was broken, and the controller asked the pilot to say again:

527: Roger, this is Cessna 527. We'd like to descend and see if we could get into VFR.

There appeared to be a fixation on going back to Ruston and a determination to descend to find VFR conditions. You need to know at this point that the flight instructor was an instrument instructor and was capable of controlling the airplane in a partial panel situation.

The heading indicator was the only gyro that failed. The accident investigation found the attitude indicator and all other instruments operating normally.

With the loss of only the heading indicator, there was no need to descend to VFR conditions. The flight could have easily continued to better weather or for an instrument approach somewhere. It wasn't necessary to find VFR conditions immediately, so the decision to descend for that purpose was a bad one.

Compass Confusion?

Within one minute of the first report of trouble, Center coordinated the return with Monroe Approach Control. The controller noticed that the Cessna's radar track had changed:

ATC: Cessna 527, are you in a turn?
527: That's negative, 527. [Was there magnetic compass confusion at work here?—Ed.]
ATC: Okay Cessna 527, you can start a right turn, right or left turn, it's your choice, and you're just outside Monroe Approach's area. Stand by just a moment.

During the next three-quarters of a minute, Center handed off the Cessna to Monroe Approach with the comment: "...[527] just wants to get to VFR and land."
     Shortly thereafter, the instructor contacted Monroe Approach Control:

ATC: Expect vectors to the Ruston Airport. The last couple people that tried to get in there could not make it VFR. Would you like the VOR DME Alpha approach? Would you be able to take that?

Determined to get VFR
Decision time again. The Cessna was not equipped with DME. The CFI acknowledged that and was still determined to get to VFR conditions:

527: Negative on the DME, just see if we can get down to a thousand.

The flight instructor's decision-making was apparently fouled by a memory of the ceiling encountered on the way out just a few minutes before. But weather moves and the lower conditions with the front had moved eastward.
     The controller was bound by the minimum IFR altitudes for the area. MEA and MOCA along Victor 94 are 2400 feet, but the minimum vectoring altitude allowed a bit of leeway:

ATC: Cessna 527, in that area descend and maintain 2000 and continue inbound. I can only take you down to 2000 in that area. Once you get down there I'll have to get your intentions then.

There was no response.

ATC: Cessna 527, did you copy?

Again, no response. The Cessna was in the trees, 440 feet above sea level.

According to the NTSB report: *The aircraft collided with high trees in a gradual, wings-level descent. The length of the wreckage distribution path and the degree of disintegration of the airframe were consistent with a relatively high airspeed.*

Descent continued

That information, plus the instructor's communications, are pretty conclusive evidence that a decision was made to continue the descent until ground contact was achieved. This decision was made in spite of information that flew in the face of such a move.

As pilots in command, we are charged with making a host of decisions on every flight. We need to fly the airplane, make a decision, and pursue the best course of action for the circumstances.

Lest we forget, let's credit the flight instructor for one very good decision on the flight. Despite the near-total destruction of the airplane as it shredded its way through the Louisiana pines, the instrument panel remained intact.

Firmly attached to the face of the failed heading indicator was a rubber suction cup that all CFIs carry to simulate instrument failure, which was placed there to reduce the distraction of the failed instrument.

• Section Four •

Disorientation

Mistaken
Identity

O ne of those nasty little details that many of us forget once we get our ratings is identifying navaids. Usually, we're using the same ones all the time, we're really too busy trying to keep up with ATC (not to mention flying the airplane) and besides, who learns Morse anymore, anyway?

Most of the time, most of us have a pretty good feel for where we are relative to the navaids on our route. But if you start following erroneous information, lose positional awareness and don't catch it, trouble is bound to catch up with you.

Making doubly sure you're tuned to the right frequency can seem trivial, but it's not. Steering off of the wrong navaid can lead at the very least to a bust, and at worst to a fatal accident.

The latter is apparently what happened to the pilot of an air ambulance in Hawaii several years ago. We don't know what actually caused this accident, but our scenario is plausible and serves to illustrate the point.

Identify That Navaid

The east slope of Kauai's Mt. Waialeala is the wettest spot on the face of the earth. Like the other Hawaiian islands, Kauai is the tip of an undersea mountain. Should you approach it from the northwest, you would see a very rapid rise in the topography from the shoreline to the summit of Mt. Waialeala, 5243 feet above the sea. When moisture-laden wind blows up that slope and dumps its load of water on the lee side, we're talking major rain forest.

It takes a great deal of shower and thunderstorm activity to support a reputation as the world's wettest place and the day of this mishap was no exception. Here's an edited excerpt from the Hawaiian Islands

Synoptic Discussion and Guidance, issued by the National Weather Service for that day: *An upper air trough is very near Kauai, and may have developed a close center. The movement which earlier appeared to be slowly eastward now appears to be slowly westward. Thunderstorms exist both north and south of Oahu and Kauai and there is a chance that these islands may receive a thunderstorm. Unstable conditions and the tradewinds which will be brought up against the windward island areas will produce some showers. A few may be heavy...in fact, a few showers may be expected almost anywhere.* (Not to impugn the weatherman, but you can hardly go wrong with your forecast when it ends with a statement like that!)

There was no rain at Honolulu International when the air ambulance pilot filed for the 40-minute flight to Lihue airport on Kauai, the first island northwest of Oahu. He filed two IFR flight plans (out and back), with a quick turnaround in Lihue...just enough time for the paramedic on the flight to load a patient and return to Honolulu. The proposed route of flight was via the Catty One Departure, then Victor 15 to Morey intersection, Victor 2 to Lihue. The flight was cleared as filed, at 6000 feet.

Pilot Familiar With Route

This pilot was no stranger to the route, the weather or the instrument approach to Kauai's primary airport. He had flown there a total of 135 times over the last 3-1/2 years, had flown at least five VOR-A approaches and had flown Seneca N2564Q to Lihue airport no less than 33 times in the last eight months. A preflight weather briefing included the probability of showers and thunderstorms.

Kauai is roughly circular. The Lihue vortac is on the airport at about the easternmost point on the island. The pilot also inquired into the status of the South Kauai VOR, ten miles southwest and near the southern shore of Kauai, which had been out of service. Today, it was reported operating normally.

At 1026 that morning, N64Q departed Runway 8L at Honolulu International, was handed-off to departure control, and eight minutes later was proceeding on course at 6000 feet, in the hands of Honolulu Center. The Piper Seneca is not a speed demon. At 1043, the following conversation took place:

Center: Six-Four-Quebec, you're being overtaken by another flight at your altitude; turn right heading 300, descend and maintain 2000 at your discretion. The Lihue altimeter is 30.07.
64Q: Okay, right to 300, descend to 2000 pilot's discretion, Lihue altimeter 30.07, Six-Four-Quebec.

At 1047:

Center: Six-Four-Quebec, turn left heading 250 for vectors around traffic. Start your descent now, maintain 3000.

64Q: Roger, left heading 250, descending to 3000.

Center: Ah Six-Four-Quebec, stop your descent at 4000.

64Q: Roger, Six-Four-Quebec, 4000.

Vector to Airway

The traffic conflict was resolved by the vectors, but N64Q was now south of the airway, which also is the final approach course for the VOR-A procedure at Lihue. At 1051, the controller issued a new heading of 320 degrees to intercept the airway. The pilot acknowledged and advised that he had slowed to 140 knots to help with the traffic problem and to get set for the approach. Three minutes later:

Center: Six-Four-Quebec, you are cleared to the Hydes intersection, hold southeast, expect further clearance at 1105.

64Q: Six-Four-Quebec is cleared to Hydes, hold southeast, expect clearance at 1105. I'm level at 4000.

Hydes is the final approach fix for the VOR-A approach to Lihue, nine miles out over the ocean between Kauai and Oahu. It's defined by the intersection of the 119° radial off Lihue and the 085 radial off South Kauai. Before he got into the holding pattern, the other airplane landed at Lihue and N64Q was cleared for the VOR-A approach. At 1103:

Center: Six-Four-Quebec, say your position.

64Q: Six-Four-Quebec, we're eleven DME.

Center: Roger Six-Four-Quebec, radar service terminated. Contact Lihue tower on 118.9.

64Q: Center, you're breaking up. Do you want me to contact Lihue tower?

Center: That's affirmative. Lihue tower on 118.9.

The frequency change was accomplished, and shortly thereafter, N64Q was talking to the local controller, who did not have the benefit of radar.

64Q: Lihue tower, Six-Four-Quebec with you on the VOR alpha approach.

Tower: Roger Six-Four-Quebec, Lihue landing runway three, wind is 040 at 12, altimeter 30.07.

64Q: Six-Four-Quebec, runway three, 30.07.

Center had other flights in the Lihue area, and since radar contact had been lost, the controller called Lihue tower on the land-line, requesting N64Q's altitude.

Tower: Six-Four-Quebec, say your altitude please.
64Q: Six-Four-Quebec passing through 3200 right now.
Tower: Roger, Six-Four-Quebec, let me know when you are out of 3000, and what is your DME at this time?
64Q: Tower, Six-Four-Quebec is out of two point five, and the DME reads ah, nine point four, nine point four.
Tower: Roger, Six-Four-Quebec, you are not in sight, cleared to land runway three.

Ten seconds later, N64Q advised that he was going around. The tower controller acknowledged the missed approach report and instructed the pilot to contact Honolulu Center on 126.5. The pilot did not acknowledge and there was no further contact.

Pilot's Thoughts?

Let's back up a bit, turn on the clairvoyance machine and join the pilot in the cockpit of the Seneca.

Okay, I'm south of Victor 2, and that 320 vector should get me back on course. Yep, there comes the needle toward center and the DME reads 18 miles.

"Six-Four-Quebec, you're cleared to the Hydes intersection, hold southeast, expect further clearance at 1105."

That's okay, I'm not there yet, Hydes is 9 DME. I'll acknowledge the holding clearance and keep motoring toward Hydes.

"Six-Four-Quebec, you are now cleared for the VOR alpha approach to Lihue. Say your position please."

Still 11 DME, didn't even get to Hydes, so I won't have to hold. That will save time. I can go straight in.

"...Lihue tower on 118.9."

Okay Center, I'll call Lihue tower...wind 040 at 12, landing runway three. Let's see now, still outside of Hydes, I can go down to 2000. Gear down, let's descend.

"Ah, tower, Six-Four-Quebec is out of 2500, DME reads nine point *four." Coming up on Hydes. There must be a fierce headwind up here. The DME is creeping toward 9.0.*

"...not in sight."

Tower doesn't have me in sight, probably due to the heavy rain, but he's cleared me to land. C'mon DME, move. Level at 2000 now, gotta hold that until Hydes. Man, there's something wrong here. I'm gonna go around. Power up, climb attitude. "Tower, Six-Four-Quebec is going around."

There might have been a quick flash of green, perhaps a sudden, subtle darkening of the gray curtain of rain just before the Seneca plowed straight ahead into the near-vertical face of Mt. Waialeala at 3000 feet. The airplane bounced and slid 300 feet down the cliff and came to rest on a small ledge. The pilot and passenger were killed instantly.

Man, Machine and Weather

There are always at least three major factors to be considered in any aircraft accident: the man, the machine and the weather. Let's look at the easy one first, the weather. The storm which swept across the Lihue airport while N64Q was executing the VOR approach was not a violent one, but the rain was heavy. Just five minutes ahead of N64Q, a Hawaiian Airlines flight was advised of 1/2 mile visibility in heavy rain showers, but the crew was able to spot the runway in time and the flight landed without incident. From the standpoints of turbulence (upsetting the airplane) or very low visibility (preventing the completion of the approach procedure from the missed approach point), weather was not a factor.

How about the machine? The Seneca was in almost daily service under FAR Part 135, which mandates rather stringent maintenance and inspection procedures. Thorough research of the airplane's records revealed nothing that would suggest system problems. The pilot was intimately familiar with N64Q and would probably have notified Center or Lihue tower if he had experienced difficulty. Airplane-wise, everything appeared completely normal and routine.

Now, the man. This is always the most difficult of the three factors to investigate, research and draw conclusions. While not a silver-haired veteran of the skies, neither was the pilot of N64Q a beginner. Seven months earlier, he completed all of the checks required by Part 135 for an IFR pilot-in-command and flew the Seneca extensively since then. His flying time totaled 1550 hours, with more than two-thirds of it multi-engine time and a couple hundred hours of IFR experience. He was a young man working his way up in the ranks of professional aviation. His skill, knowledge and attitude were praised by those who knew him.

Perhaps the recorded radar information provides the best clue to the cause of this accident. Although the Enroute Automated Radar Tracking System at Honolulu Center was in operation that day, it had not been commissioned and the accuracy of the recorded information could not be verified. Assuming that what appeared on the radar records was at least reasonably correct, an interesting pattern appears.

At about 1102, when the Seneca was cleared for the approach, the radar plot shows the flight 1/2 mile *west* of the Lihue vortac—the pilot was already over land! At 1103, when the controller requested a position report, the pilot responded eleven miles, but the radar plot shows 1-3/4 miles *west* of the vortac. (Remember, the pilot was waiting for the DME to count down to 9.0, identifying Hydes, the final approach fix and the point from which he could descend from 2000 feet.)

At 1105, radar shows N64Q 7-1/2 miles from the vortac, still proceeding westbound and well inland, waiting for Hydes, and at 1106, the airplane was 9.6 miles west of Lihue. When queried, the pilot said that his distance was 9.4 miles and the missed approach was commenced shortly thereafter. The impact point was ten miles west of the vortac, on the Lihue 229 radial, the reciprocal of the final approach course. The pilot had evidently flown right over the field.

Do you recall earlier when we mentioned the pilot's preflight inquiry about the South Kauai VOR? If you would like to play accident investigator for a moment, consider that an 11-mile arc drawn from the South Kauai vortac (SOK) through its northeast quadrant comes close to the final approach course for Lihue. Further, recall that the Seneca was south of the final approach course.

Now visualize an airplane flying inbound from south of the airway to intercept the LIH 119 radial (final approach course), with the DME tuned to SOK. A pretty good demonstration of flying a DME arc, but unfortunately very misleading for the pilot.

If this indeed is what happened, it explains why the DME reading moved so slowly toward nine miles. It probably explains why N64Q flew and flew until the pilot sensed that something was very wrong. It explains why the impact occurred where it did, but it does not explain why the pilot would allow himself to become so confused and misled by conflicting navigation indications.

Cause Unknown

The actual cause of this crash was never determined, and it never will be. As always, there are lessons to be learned to avoid a similar occurrence.

Perhaps the most obvious and important lesson is to never rely on navigation information you haven't checked and rechecked. Your airplane might not have an audio selector panel which permits identification of a DME signal. Nonetheless, be sure you know where the distance information is coming from, especially if that information is critical to the procedure, as in this case. As you get into fancier airplanes with more bells and whistles in the avionics department, the chances of programming and/or reading wrong information increase remarkably.

Second, pay close attention to the primary navaid when flying an approach procedure in weather. If this pilot had noticed the reversal of the to/from indicator when he crossed the Lihue vortac, he would have known that the DME information was correct.

Positional Awareness Important

Third, be very aware of your position at all times when flying inside a cloud. Maintain a sense of how rapidly things are moving. When the timing doesn't seem right (that DME is *creeping* toward 9.0.), there's most likely a good reason for it. Figure it out, or go around.

The pilot of N64Q finally got the message, but it was too late.

We have taken considerable liberties with our recounting of this accident, e.g., radio communications have been highly edited and our short trip inside the pilot's mind is pure speculation. In any event, we offer this recounting for the sole purpose of helping you know more about instrument flying, to recognize some of the traps that lie in wait for all pilots, and hopefully, to prevent another occurrence like this one.

Confused
and Disoriented

One of the most confusing areas of learning for beginning instrument pilots is the relationship between VOR radials and courses. When you're outbound from a VOR, the radial and course are the same and when you're inbound to a VOR, they're opposites.

Once you get the two confused, it's awfully easy to get good and lost. Certain equipment can make the task much easier. One of our favorite gadgets, the HSI, is a tremendous help here.

The pilot of the Baron in this accident had one, but it was not working. It's possible that the lack of an easily interpreted "crutch" may have contributed to his confusion.

This accident involves confusion over VOR radials, as well as the ability to understand a controller's clearance.

Which Way to Atlanta?

Weather in the southeastern U.S. on this October day was IMC. A tropical storm was in the northern Gulf of Mexico and its easterly winds moved moisture across Georgia, generating cloud layers from 600 to 22,000 feet.

Visibility along the route from St. Simons Island to Atlanta was three miles in fog and rain. A pilot who flew the same route as the accident airplane reported that he was in the clouds the entire trip, but did not encounter turbulence. This was not a bad day for a relatively new instrument pilot to acquire some wet time.

The pilot was a successful doctor. He learned to fly in Switzerland and continued his flight training in the U.S. as his practice permitted.

He progressed fairly rapidly. He obtained a U.S. private pilot certificate (based on his Swiss license) in October, 1983, an instrument rating in August, 1984 and a commercial certificate in April, 1985. The instrument and commercial were obtained in his A36 Bonanza. Three months later, he acquired a multi-engine rating in a Beech Baron.

The doctor had approximately 450 hours, with 93 hours in the Baron, 48 hours at night, 58 hours in actual IFR conditions and 32 hours of hood time.

The accident airplane was a Beech Baron 58P (pressurized), which the doctor purchased three months earlier. He attended the Beech ground school for the airplane. His flight instructor, who completed the program with him, commented that the pilot was attentive during the majority of the course, but did not complete homework assignments.

The instructor stated that the pilot "...appeared more infatuated with his radar and avionics than with acquiring knowledge of the airplane." The Baron had all the bells and whistles.

One of the pilot's colleagues believed he was "...moving too rapidly and acquiring advanced ratings with insufficient experience and moving into aircraft with too much performance too quickly."

The Flight

The pilot departed McKinnon Airport on St. Simons Island, Georgia for his home base at Peachtree-DeKalb Airport, just north of Atlanta. N583AM was cleared via Victor 179 to the Husky Intersection, then direct Peachtree at 12,000 feet. (See the accompanying chart excerpt).

Everything went well until the Baron neared Rippi Intersection (Point #1 on the chart). ATC descended N83AM to 10,000 feet and we join the communication as the controller issues another descent:

ATC: Baron Eight-Three-Alpha-Mike, descend and maintain seven thousand.
N83AM: Alpha-Mike, down to seven.

Radar data showed N83AM descending at 500 feet per minute on the centerline of the airway. The pilot flew this route often and was aware that a northwesterly track was necessary to his destination (keep that in mind). At this point, N82AM was southeast of Husky Intersection.

Unusual Request

Five minutes later (Point #2), the controller was aware of a traffic conflict:

ATC: Baron Eight-Three-Alpha-Mike, I'm gonna have to make a right

360 with you for spacing into Atlanta. If you'll give me about, ah, five miles on the downwind leg, I'll be able to turn you back in. Descend and maintain five thousand, make a right 360.
N83AM: Okay, down to five thousand and a 360 to the right.
ATC: And just give me about five miles on the downwind leg, and ah, we'll have plenty of separation for you.

The controller's request was far from standard. You won't find that phraseology in the controller's handbook. It's difficult to imagine a 360-degree turn with a five-mile downwind leg.FAR 91.75 requires a pilot to ask for clarification if uncertain about a clearance. The pilot should have responded to the controller's instruction with, "I can do either of those, but not both. Which do you want?"

Confusion Reigns
Radar data indicated that the pilot executed a 360. The pilot was three-quarters through the turn (Point #3) when:

ATC: And Baron Eight-Three-Alpha-Mike, you can turn back inbound and ah join the Atlanta 128 radial, Husky, direct Peachtree-Dekalb.
N83AM: Okay, ah, 180 radial and then ah Peachtree direct. Is that correct? [No, that's not correct!]

The controller corrected the misunderstanding:

ATC: Roger, the 128 radial Husky and then direct.

The pilot was close, but he still didn't get it right:

N83AM: Okay, the 120 radial to Husky then direct.

The controller left the error unchallenged.
Four minutes passed, during which the Baron tracked very close to the airway, but headed southeast (Point #4). The controller noticed that something was amiss (four minutes later?) and inquired:

ATC: [Knowing very well what his heading is] Ah, Eight-Three-Alpha-Mike, what's your heading now?
N83AM: Ah, my heading is ah, 128. I have a malfunction in my autopilot system, so I am flying via the second VHR [sic].

If some of that explanation doesn't make sense, remember the pilot was

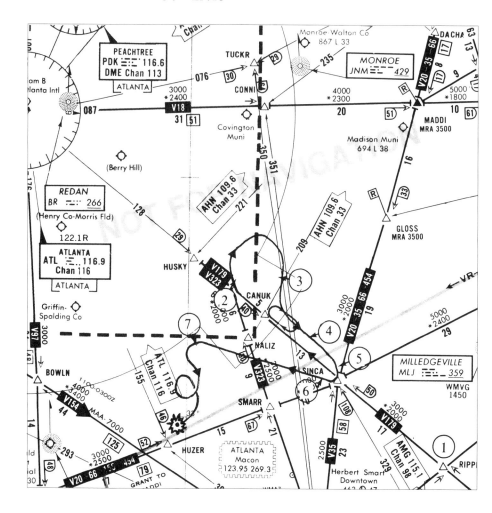

The Baron was cleared via Victor 179 to Husky, then direct Peachtree-Dekalb. Everything went smoothly for the pilot until reaching Rippi, when the controller asked him to make a right 360 with a five-mile downwind leg.

Swiss. Although he had mastered English, there were some aeronautical terms that didn't come out the way they were intended. Investigators believed he meant he was navigating with the second VOR. An autopilot malfunction was considered unlikely, but was never determined.

Directional Awareness Lost

An awareness of his position and the controller's instruction to turn back inbound now could only mean a turn to the northwest. The pilot was obviously confused between the course and the radial. The #1 nav was an HSI and the #2 nav was a standard VOR display. Setting either nav to the wrong heading could result in course and TO/FROM indications that would require considerable interpretation.

It's difficult to comprehend why the pilot would fly a heading of 128 when he must have known a northwest heading was necessary. His mention of a failed autopilot raised the possibility of a failed heading card, but you wouldn't expect a pilot of this experience to maintain a heading of precisely 128 degrees by using only the magnetic compass.

At Point #5, the Baron leveled at 5000 feet, having descended at a consistent rate. The controller vectored him to 300°. N83AM complied (Point #6), and three minutes later, with the airplane headed in the right direction, the controller issued a new clearance: "And Baron Eight-Three-Alpha-Mike, just proceed direct Norcross, direct Peachtree-Dekalb."

The clearance to Norcross VOR (ten miles northwest of Peachtree-Dekalb) was acknowledged by the pilot.

Equipment Failure?

The radar track showed that the Baron was drifting more and more to the west (Point #7), and after two minutes, the controller asked:

ATC: And ah, Eight-Three-Alpha-Mike, are you back on autopilot again? You're headed south.
N83AM: No, ah, negative. I have to fly with my RMI backup. The autopilot and the whole first system is gone.
ATC: Okay, fly heading 340, heading 340.
N83AM: 340, okay.

The Baron also had an RMI; it is a second heading card slaved to the HSI. The RMI displays the same heading as the HSI, but instead, has two pointers, one for the ADF and one for the #1 VOR.

If the heading cards malfunctioned and froze, the pointers would still provide correct magnetic course information, albeit in the wrong place on the card.

Investigators looked very closely at the confusion this might create, e.g., if the heading cards failed during the first turn (Point #1) and locked on a heading of northeast, the VOR pointer on the RMI would have shown the Norcross VOR to the left of the nose when the airplane was heading 300°. Various combinations of failed heading cards and VOR selections were considered, but no agreement was reached as to what actually happened.

The investigators also considered the possibility that the nav system worked properly and the errant track of the Baron was due to a completely confused pilot, whose problems began with a turn in the wrong direction at Point #3.

For whatever reason, N83AM turned left when the controller asked him to turn right to a heading of 340°. The turn continued through two short-radius 360s with a 500-foot variation in altitude. Nothing more was heard from the pilot. The Baron hit the ground with such force that both engines were buried two feet in the Georgia soil.

NTSB Decides

No one will ever know exactly what happened. The NTSB determined the probable causes were, aircraft handling—not maintained—pilot in command, and improper use of equipment/spatial disorientation—pilot in command.

This pilot was trained to use his flight instruments and navigational equipment in normal operations and emergencies. He was familiar with the equipment in the Baron since his former airplane (the A36 Bonanza) was similarly equipped.He obviously controlled the airplane quite well to the end, even though he flew in the wrong direction at the outset. So why didn't he continue with the controller's vectors?

Lessons Learned

In this case, a misinterpretation appears to be the beginning of monumental confusion.

We've said this before, but when things don't seem right, they probably aren't. When a controller asks, What's your heading?, you should immediately assess the situation. Challenge any clearance or instruction that doesn't make sense.

Whenever you find yourself in strange waters, e.g., disorientation, navigation confusion, aircraft system problems, the best course of action is to request and fly straight and level for a few minutes until you get things sorted out.

There's nothing more important to a pilot than keeping the airplane under control.

The Drum
DG Trap

The first report of trouble before an aircraft accident occurs sometimes leads investigators in the wrong direction, until more information comes to light. The pilot told controllers that he was having trouble with the airplane, but what may be the real underlying cause of the crash wasn't apparent until after the investigation was well underway.

This is another accident with many underlying causes, including lack of currency unfamiliarity with the airplane's handling, and lack of currency. Perhaps most important, however, is the distinct possibility of confusion and disorientation caused by the pilot's lack of experience with the airplane's old-fashioned drum-style heading indicator.

What Was the Real Problem?

On a foggy July morning, the pilot of a Piper Comanche intended a business trip from Atlanta's Peachtree-Dekalb Airport to Anderson, South Carolina. He got weather briefings the night before and 90 minutes before takeoff.

The Atlanta area was an island of low ceilings and visibilities that morning, with 300 overcast and three miles in fog and haze. Athens, Georgia (45 miles to the east) was also wrapped in fog, but most other airports southeast of Atlanta were considerably better, with ceilings of at least 8000 feet and visibilities of four miles or better.

The previous night's briefing had indicated that Atlanta and Anderson would improve after 9 a.m., but that there was a chance of partial obscuration and visibility one-half mile in fog in the Anderson area until 10 a.m.

The forecast was accurate, as evidenced in the morning briefing.

Anderson reported 500 broken (no visibility) and Greenville-Spartanburg (30 miles from Anderson) was 100 overcast and 1/4 mile in fog. No improvement was expected until noon and scattered thunderstorms were reported along the route. This briefing was enough for any single-engine pilot to think twice about launching into IMC.

Nevertheless, business called and the Comanche departed at 8:28 a.m. The weather was 300 overcast, three miles in fog and haze. All went well until 8:40 a.m., when the pilot told Atlanta Center, "...we'd like to go back to Peachtree, we're having a little, ah, alternator or generator trouble."

The controller immediately cleared the Comanche direct to Norcross VOR, then direct Peachtree. The radar target showed a turn toward the VOR and the flight was handed off to Atlanta Approach. The controller told the pilot to maintain 5000 feet and to expect the ILS Runway 20L at Peachtree.

Communications were less than ideal as the flight proceeded toward the VOR. The pilot reported having radio problems (reception was broken) and he was in heavy rain. Nothing was heard from the Comanche for two minutes. Then the pilot said, "You're all right, we're just getting a drain on our batteries. We'd like direct as possible back to Peachtree."

At 8:49, the Comanche was cleared down to 3000 feet. The pilot acknowledged this and vectors until he was almost lined up with the localizer.

At 8:53, the controller told him to "Turn left heading 200, intercept the localizer, cleared for the ILS Runway 20L approach."

The pilot did not acknowledge this or three subsequent transmissions.

At 8:54, he said, "Ah, tower, you're garbled..."

Things were getting tight. The Comanche was over the outer marker, heading southwest, and not in position for the approach. Recognizing the situation, the controller said, "Turn left heading 180. You're at the marker now, ah, and intercept the localizer...or do you want to come out and try another shot at it?"

The pilot responded, "We'd like to try to shoot it." The clearance was repeated, but the pilot didn't respond to that or any further transmissions.

Radar data showed that the Comanche went through the localizer from east to west about one mile outside the marker. Perhaps more significant, the airplane turned left to 180 degrees, then turned northward and slightly westward in the last 30 seconds before radar contact was lost.

People on the ground reported seeing and hearing the Comanche flying in low clouds at treetop level. The engine was reported running smoothly even after power was reduced just before impact. The airplane crashed into a level field in an inverted, nose-low attitude. The pilot was killed.

Electrical Trouble

The pilot had purchased the Comanche only ten days before the accident. During his first trip, the electrical system failed and required an emergency gear extension.

A passenger on that flight reported that the pilot was constantly playing with the circuit breakers under the left side of the instrument panel. The passenger believed electrical power was restored due to the pilot's check of the circuit breakers.

Following this incident, the pilot took the airplane to a repair shop at Peachtree Airport. He reported that the landing gear circuit breaker had popped and the ammeter showed a high battery discharge. A mechanic checked the generator and voltage regulator, reset the generator output voltage, and found all other electrical system operations normal.

Even though this airplane was dependent on electricity for operation of the landing gear and radios, loss of electrical power need not have resulted in disaster, since flight controls and vacuum-powered instruments weren't affected.

It appeared that only communications were affected by an electrical problem. This was supported by radar returns, which continued to the very end, an indication that the transponder worked just fine.

The investigation shifted to other factors that may have contributed to this accident.

Takeoff Questionable

The pilot's decision to depart in the first place was reviewed. FAR 91 operators do not have instrument takeoff minimums and can legally depart in zero-zero conditions.

But if you're flying a single-engine airplane and develop engine trouble, there are no approaches that permit zero-visibility landings.

In this case, if the pilot believed he absolutely had to fly to Anderson that morning, he might have considered one of the other airports in the area with better weather as a takeoff alternate. The attempted return to Peachtree was probably not a good idea.

Pilot Proficiency

Another factor was the pilot's proficiency. He was a 33-year old private pilot with 742 hours and an instrument rating. He had flown 7.8 hours in the Comanche in the preceding ten days, but none of it in instrument conditions.

In the preceding six months, the pilot logged only four instrument approaches, all of them during an IFR recurrency training flight. The flight instructor who conducted the training believed the pilot was not proficient enough to be endorsed for an instrument competency check.

According to the instructor, the pilot was rusty on instruments, had difficulty on the instrument approaches, was poor on intercepting radials and was unable to stay on the localizer during an approach to Runway 20L at Peachtree-Dekalb.

When the pilot lowered the gear at the outer marker, he completely lost the glideslope. The instructor discussed the need for additional training with him, but the pilot never found the time to do it.

Perhaps the most telling factor of all was revealed by the man who sold the airplane. This Comanche had one of the old drum-type heading indicators. The salesman/check pilot said this baffled the new owner during his checkout flight.

With the old-style heading indicator, there is no depiction of the airplane on a flat card. Instead, you look through a small window at a portion of a horizontal card. It's the same view you have of the magnetic compass card and the headings appear to increase and decrease in the wrong direction.

A pilot using this heading indicator must decide which way to turn before moving the controls. It takes time and practice to make using this instrument second nature.

It's possible this pilot (baffled by the heading indicator) was confused as the localizer needle moved rapidly across the CDI and turned the wrong way. He may have realized his mistake and made a steep disorienting turn to correct the error.

This scenario raises another factor, the problem of a non-stabilized approach. A good instrument approach is like a paint job. The last coat (the one that shows) is only as good as the underlying coats. A good final approach (the one that counts) is only as good as the procedure leading up to the final approach fix.

This pilot was properly vectored to the approach, but apparently lost heading control. He lost control of the airplane while attempting to regain the localizer from an unusual position.

A stabilized approach is one in which the airplane is established on the localizer at the proper distance for glideslope intercept, at the proper airspeed, in the proper configuration, and set to lower the gear at glideslope intercept.

Anything but stabilized is a good reason to fly the missed approach procedure and come back for a better attempt.

Important Lessons

Five important lessons emerge from this accident:

• 1. Think twice about leaping into near- or below-minimum conditions in any airplane, especially a single-engine.

• 2. Have a solid-gold alternate for every phase of flight, including takeoff, even if the alternate is nothing more than a heading to better weather.

• 3. When a problem rears its ugly head, comply with aviation rule #1, which is, *fly the airplane.*

• 4. Make every instrument approach a stabilized approach and go around if it becomes unstabilized.

• 5. Get yourself comfortably current and proficient before attempting actual instrument conditions and do whatever is necessary to stay that way.

Disorientation
In the Dark

Y ou've just missed your second ILS approach in low
IMC at night after a five-hour flight. You're being
vectored for another approach, when suddenly you
find yourself having to recover from an unusual attitude. Now imagine all this
happening while at the controls of a DC-8. While this sounds too horrible to
be true, it actually happened to an experienced flight crew.

Although the National Transportation Safety Board (NTSB) determined
the cause of this accident was the failure of the flight crew to properly recognize
or recover in a timely manner from the unusual aircraft attitude that resulted
from the captain's apparent spatial disorientation, fatigue and wind shear
were also present in the events leading to the accident.

The Hazards of Night IFR

ATI Flight 805 was an air freighter operating under FAR 121 on a
regularly scheduled route from Portland, OR to Seattle, WA and then
on to Toledo, OH. The flight departed Portland at 9:45 p.m. EST. After
landing at Seattle, freight was unloaded and loaded and AT805 departed at 11:20 p.m. The trip was uneventful until arriving in the
Toledo area at 3:00 a.m., where IFR conditions prevailed.

As they were being vectored by Toledo Approach, the crew picked
up the current ATIS:

Measured ceiling 500 broken, 1700 broken, 2500 overcast, visibility
two and one half, light rain, light drizzle and fog. Temperature 34,
dewpoint 32, wind 100 at 12, altimeter 2981. ILS Runway 7 approach in
use. Notice to airmen, approach lights for Runway 7 are out of service...

At 3:07, AT805 was 23 nm from the outer marker and assigned a heading of 100 to intercept the localizer.

ATC: Maintain 2300 until established on the localizer, cleared for the approach.

The captain acknowledged and got the following from the controller:

ATC: We're on level one and level two precipitation echoes along the final approach course and although the other guys went through, I didn't have any complaints. I had reports earlier of light rain.

At this point, the cockpit voice recorder (CVR) reflects a discussion between the captain (Capt) and first officer (FO) about their assigned altitude. This was a precursor of how things would go for the approach, which the first officer flew:

FO: We're cleared to 2400 [feet], is that correct?
Capt: If I were you I would stay here at 4000 until we intercept the glideslope...can't go down cause you don't know where you are.
FO: Right. I thought she [the controller] cleared us to 2400 and cleared us for the approach?
Capt: No, I didn't hear the 2400. There, the localizer's coming alive anyway. Now you can go down. [Three minutes earlier, the captain had acknowledged the approach clearance with an assigned altitude of 2300 feet.—Ed.]

The crew completed the approach checklist. When the first officer called for gear down, before landing check, the captain responded with need some more flaps. The CVR then reflects the sound of the flap lever being activated, followed by the gear warning horn. The sound of the flap lever is heard again, followed by the captain saying, "Where the **** is it?"

He was either trying to locate the detent for the flap lever or the gear handle. In either case, the gear lowered seconds later. Was the captain feeling the effects of fatigue and/or the wee hours of the morning? More on this later.

AT805 was cleared to land with the wind 100 degrees at 9. The first officer was having difficulty getting stabilized on both the localizer and glideslope. This prompted the following commentary by the captain:

Capt: You still don't have enough flaps for this speed...add power...you're not on the glidepath...bring it up to the glidepath. You're not even on the #### localizer at all. Something's bad wrong, keep the speed up. Okay, we're gonna have to go around cause we're not anywhere near the localizer...anywhere near it.

The crew initiated a missed approach and was handed off to Toledo Approach:

App: AT805 heavy, radar contact at 2600. What was wrong?
Capt: We lost the localizer close in there...couldn't position ourselves on final...we had the glidepath but not the localizer.

AT805 was vectored to the west for another shot at the ILS. The first officer was still flying and the cockpit conversation took on an interesting demeanor; like a discussion between a flight instructor and an instrument student. As they were being vectored, the captain kept reassuring the first officer:

Capt: You're flying at 2300 [feet], so you're okay and heading downwind now....

When they were six miles from the outer marker, Approach gave the crew a heading of 100 to intercept the localizer at 2300 feet and cleared them for the ILS. As the localizer came on-scale, the captain commented:

Capt: We're gonna have trouble with the right drift here...let's see what it looks like.

Approach called and told AT805 to contact the tower, which the captain acknowledged. He then commented to the first officer:

Capt: It's gonna take quite a bit of drift there because you got 14 degrees of left drift...it takes a lot...the wind's blowing like a #### up here.

One minute later, the captain observed: 13 degrees of left drift...man they really got a bad #### situation here...right out of the south direct crosswind giving you 12 degrees of drift right now.

This prompted a call to the tower:
Capt: What are your winds down there now tower?
Tower: 100 at 10.
Capt: Okay, up here on the final approach course you got winds at 180 at about 35 knots.

The captain returned to coaching the first officer: Don't take too much out. You need to hold it in there for awhile. Still asking for a right turn but don't get slow because you got plenty of wind down here to help you.

This was followed by the sound of increased engine power. The crew then got three sink rate and two glideslope warnings.

Capt: Push the power and get it back up to the glidepath...Okay now take it off...stay with it.

With the first officer again failing to stabilize the approach, the captain took the controls and initiated a missed approach. The first officer called the tower:

FO: 805 is on the missed.
Tower: AT805, climb and maintain 3000...new Toledo weather for 805 heavy is measured 400 overcast, visibility 2 miles with light rain and fog...AT805 heavy, turn left heading 300.

The flight data recorder (FDR) shows the airplane leveled at 3200 feet on a northeasterly heading. As the captain turned left to comply with the assigned heading, the bank angle increased to almost 60° and he remarked, "What the ####s the matter here?"

He appeared to be confused about the airplane's attitude. The captain turned to the first officer and said, "You got it?" The first officer acknowledged and took the controls. With the bank angle increasing to 80°, the airplane was descending in a 30-degree nose-down attitude.

The first officer rolled in the opposite direction to level the wings, but the airplane was still descending and the altitude and sink rate warnings sounded. "Pull up!" exclaimed the flight engineer. The ground proximity warning system (GPWS) sounded: *Pull up! Pull up! Pull up!*

The flight engineer again exclaimed, "Pull up!" Again the GPWS sounded: *Pull up! Pull up! Pull up!*

Then the captain commanded, "Up up up up." Just before impact, the captain again commanded, "Up up."

AT805 hit the ground at more than 300 knots in a 20-degree left bank and 17° nose-down. No one survived.

Contributing Factors

The ensuing investigation reviewed a number of possible contributors to this accident and zeroed-in on fatigue, wind shear, spatial disorientation and the possibility of attitude indicator failure.

Although NTSB couldn't prove it conclusively, there were signs that fatigue could have played a role in this accident. The crew departed Portland at 9:45 p.m. EST, which means they would have reported for duty earlier for a weather briefing, preflight, etc. They arrived in the Toledo more than five hours later (at 3:00 a.m.) to tackle an approach with a 400-foot ceiling, two miles visibility in rain, fog and with the approach lights out of service; not the most ideal conditions for the end of a long trip. As they were cleared for the first approach, the captain said he didn't hear the controller clear them down to 2300 feet. Not remembering the details of a clearance during a long flight is a sign you aren't as sharp as you should be. The crew also missed some standard call-outs during both approaches and never completed the approach checklist before their second approach.

The first officer's poor performance during the two approaches could also have been influenced by fatigue. He must have been wrung out by the time the captain took the controls after the second failed approach. It must have surprised the first officer to suddenly have the controls back during the second missed approach when the captain apparently got disoriented. During the few moments it took for the first officer to recognize the unusual attitude and initiate a recovery, the bank angle increased to 80° and the pitch decreased to 30° nose- down. That's a scary scenario in instrument conditions at night.

Vexing Winds

The weather systems that night consisted of a low pressure area over western Illinois with a warm front extending eastward through southern Ohio. Although there were airmets for occasional moderate icing below 18,000 feet and occasional moderate turbulence below 12,000 feet, no one reported problems with ice or turbulence during approaches into Toledo that night.

There were, however, some interesting low-level winds that obviously plagued the DC-8 crew during their two approaches. While the surface wind seemed benign (100 degrees at 10), here's what the National Weather Service upper air data revealed:

- 2000 feet - 195° @ 31 kts
- 3000 feet - 210° @ 35 kts
- 4000 feet - 225° @ 39 kts
- 5000 feet - 234° @ 37 kts

As the crew flew the first approach, they encountered a right-quartering tailwind of more than 30 knots that became a direct right-crosswind at the outer marker, which then became a right- quartering headwind on the ground. That's a situation requiring advance planning and skill to handle.

The crew must have been surprised at what they thought was going to be a routine ILS. There wasn't any convective activity present and they had a smooth ride. The low-level wind shear alerting system at Toledo didn't indicate the presence of wind shear on the surface.

NTSB investigators interviewed flight crews from other aircraft that flew the approach before the accident flight. The captain of another DC-8 reported, The approach down final was a little bumpy with shifting winds, but manageable. He saw the runway at 300 feet and estimated the forward visibility as one to one and a half miles. Other crews reported using from 10 to 25 degrees of right crab to track the localizer at altitude and a high descent rate (1100 fpm) when intercepting the glideslope, but were able to successfully complete the approach.

There's no doubt shear conditions existed on the approach. Again, you have to wonder if the first officer had difficulty handling the approach due to fatigue.

Gyro Failure

NTSB also considered the possibility that the captain's attitude indicator (AI) failed during the second missed approach. The AI was recovered from the wreckage and examined, but there was no conclusive evidence it had malfunctioned. Additionally, a review of maintenance records didn't reveal any recorded deficiencies with the instrument.

The Safety Board also reviewed FAA Service Difficulty Reports and found 36 reports of problems with the same type of attitude gyro used in the accident airplane. In some instances, there were conflicting indications in the pilot and co-pilot displays and failures that occurred without instrument failure flags coming into view.

In this case, there was nothing said by either pilot that indicated an instrument problem. Although it took him a moment to figure things out, the first officer was executing the proper recovery for an unusual attitude from a descent by first leveling the wings and then raising the pitch. NTSB concluded that a problem with the captain's gyro was feasible, but couldn't be proven.

Spatial Disorientation

Just before the captain turned over aircraft control to the first officer, his comment (What's the matter?) could indicate he was confused. In its report, NTSB stated:

Although the captain was routinely turning to the assigned heading of 300 degrees when control was lost, he had just transitioned from a climb, reduced power and was still attempting to level at the assigned altitude of 3000 feet. This combination of steady, sustained turning, acceleration-to-deceleration changeover and abrupt ascent to descent transition, at night with no visible horizon or outside references is especially conducive to spatial disorientation...It is also known that fatigue increases pilot susceptibility to disorientation and decreases the ability to cope after disorientation. Therefore, the Safety Board believes that many of the events and circumstances of this accident strongly point to a conclusion that the captain experienced spatial disorientation.

No Respect

This accident certainly makes a good case for maintaining proficiency at unusual attitude recovery. When close to the ground, prompt recognition of the problem, followed by an aggressive recovery is all-important. If you're accustomed to conducting proficiency training during the day, go up some night with an instructor and review unusual attitude recoveries, partial panel approaches and other situations that can induce vertigo. Spatial disorientation doesn't respect a pilot's age, certificates nor hours. In this case, the captain had more than 16,000 hours and the first officer had more than 5000 hours.

Insidious Fatigue

Even though this crew was experienced in night air cargo operations, they weren't immune from the insidious effects of fatigue. If you've ever flown when tired, you know the tell-tale signs that your performance is going downhill: missing items in a clearance, fixating on instruments instead of scanning and not following the checklist. Acknowledging the fact you might be fatigued is precisely when you should religiously adhere to the checklist, copy and readback all clearance items and force yourself to maintain a proper scan pattern.

Your preflight planning should include an assessment of the conditions en route and how sharp you'll be to fly an approach to minimums at your destination.

Wind Shear Warning

Wind shear doesn't occur only around convective weather. Anytime there's a strong wind at low altitude, be alert for a shear condition during climb after takeoff or during descent for an approach. Compare the winds on the surface with those aloft. If the surface wind is light and the winds at 3000 feet are much stronger and vary 90 degrees or more from those on the surface, expect a suddenly shift from a tailwind to a headwind or vice versa.

Autopilot Assist

We don't know why the captain didn't elect to fly an autopilot coupled approach at the first sign of trouble. This would have been the best course of action after a long and grueling flight.

When all else fails and you don't feel comfortable with the approach you're about to fly or at any time during the approach, go to your alternate or anywhere else more favorable conditions exist.

Doubly Lost

Two heads are better than one is an often heard saying when it comes to problem solving. Two heads in the cockpit can be better than one, provided both pilots understand how to work together as a team.

But when both members of the flight crew are lost, their confusion tends to compound itself, making the situation worse, not better.

This accident, the crash of a Beech 99 commuter, resulted when the two-pilot crew lost positional awareness after they were cleared for an ILS approach. There are several important lessons from this accident for both single- and two-pilot operators about the need to maintain positional awareness, use all available resources during an approach and be prepared for weather surprises.

Are Two Heads Better?

This was the first day of a new route for the commuter airline. It was also the first day for the newly hired captain as an airline pilot. The first officer had been working for the operator for one month. Neither pilot had flown this route before in the Beech 99, nor had they ever flown together.

Flight 861 departed Atlanta, GA at 8:22 on a June morning, headed for Anniston, AL (75 nm west of Atlanta) with four passengers. The captain was flying, while the first officer handled communication and navigation responsibilities. Atlanta Departure cleared the flight to 6000 feet and assigned a heading of 280, which paralleled north of V-18 between Atlanta and Talladega VOR. The airplane was equipped with a cockpit voice recorder, so we have the benefit of cockpit conversation.

Their conversation revealed they were IMC and evaluating some convective activity along their route with onboard radar. They had been on the 280-heading for some time when the captain asked:

Capt: Does this vector intercept an airway?
FO: It looks like it's coming in real slow.

His response didn't inform the captain about what they were intercepting.

At 8:40 a.m., the flight was talking to Atlanta Center and was cleared down to 5000 feet.

Capt: Does he want us to resume our own navigation? queried the captain, As far as I'm concerned, I'm still on vectors 280.
FO: Two-eight-zero's fine. We're on course anyway so let's just hold it.

Again, not a descriptive response of what on course meant.

Their continued discussion indicated the captain was confused about their position. The first officer's answers didn't seem to clarify the captain's confusion:

Capt: We're slowly drifting off.
FO: Turn that 085 to the course.
Capt: What's the course?
FO: 085 inbound. [This is the airway radial from TDG VOR—Ed.]
Capt: You mean 065?

They were north of V18, roughly paralleling it. At this point tracking the 065 radial inbound would probably have taken them to the VOR.

FO: 085 (pause) 085.
Capt: Then we're way off course.
FO: East is 090.

Their discussion was cut off by a call from Center:

Center: 861, radar service is terminated, contact Birmingham Approach 125.45.

The first officer acknowledged, called Birmingham Approach and got the following response:

Approach: 861, descend and maintain 4000 and continue direct

Talladega. If you're unable to get the Anniston Airport in sight, expect no delay for the ILS 5 from over Bogga. There is an area of weather southwest of Bogga on the final approach course about four to five miles. Anniston's reporting 1500 scattered, estimated ceiling 10,000 broken, visibility 5 with light rain, fog and haze. The wind 060 at 6.

This was the first time ATC had told the flight to proceed direct Talladega. Also, the Birmingham controller never told the crew they were in radar contact (more on this later).

The first officer acknowledged the clearance, then:

Capt: Okay, right now we're tracking direct to the Talladega VOR.
FO: That's correct. [They were still north of V-18.—Ed.]

The crew was setting up for the approach when ATC called:

Approach: 861, new Anniston weather 700 scattered, estimated ceiling 1500 broken, 9000 overcast, 3 miles in fog and haze. The 700-foot layer is scattered variable to broken; appears to be breaking up. The wind is 090 at 5.

The first officer acknowledged and asked the captain if he wanted to go around for the ILS. Before the captain could respond:

Approach: 861, proceed direct Bogga. Maintain 4000 until Bogga, cleared ILS Runway 5 approach.

The clearance was acknowledged, then:
Capt: Ask him distance from...
FO: From Bogga?
Capt: That's okay, I'll just...
FO: We're ah...minus six point one. We're five miles from Bogga.

To figure the distance from Bogga, the first officer probably noted the distance from TDG to Bogga (6.1 miles) on the approach chart and subtracted that from the current DME reading. The first officer apparently believed they were five miles east of Bogga, when in fact they were about four miles northeast of the airport (see the accompanying radar track).

The workload and confusion only got worse from this point, which prompted the captain to comment:

Capt: Well, it's all kind of ganged up here on me a little fast. Think we're goin' to go through it. [The localizer—Ed.]

Their discussion continued to indicate doubt about their position:

Capt: I bet you. I think we're right over the outer...
FO: We're right over Bogga. He kept us in real tight. I mean God we're, we're four and a half out. That was uncalled for. Go ahead and drop your gear, speed checks.
Capt: Glideslope isn't even alive. (pause) What's the minimum altitude I can descend to until I'm established?
FO: Until established, 2200. [The chart shows glideslope intercept at 2200 feet just before Bogga.—Ed.]

There's no evidence the crew ever tuned and identified the LOM. Instead, they must have mistakenly believed they were directly east of Bogga. The absent glideslope indication should've been a further warning that something was amiss. The radar track shows the crew flew through the Runway 5 localizer northeast of the runway. They then flew a course reversal until crossing the localizer again, at which point the crew turned to intercept what they believed to be the inbound course to Runway 5.

Just before intercepting the localizer, the captain said, "We gotta go missed on this."

Executing the missed approach at this point would probably have saved the day, but the first officer talked him out of it and they actually tracked the localizer away from the field.

The final moments of cockpit conversation reveals an unstabilized approach as the captain hurriedly descended to the glideslope intercept altitude of 2200 feet, with a continued descent to reach the localizer MDA of 1100 feet. There was one more exchange about why the glideslope wasn't working and the location of the missed approach point before the aircraft crashed in a heavily wooded area 7.5 miles northeast of the airport at 1800 feet msl. The terrain was obscured by fog and low clouds. The captain and two passengers died. The first officer and two other passengers were seriously injured.

Crew Training Reviewed

During the investigation, NTSB reviewed the qualifications and training of the two pilots and why the commuter airline paired them together for this flight. The captain was a former U.S. Army helicopter pilot and flight instructor with more than 1600 hours of helicopter time that included the UH-60 Blackhawk (which is twin-engine turbine-powered). After leaving active duty, he was a full-time civilian flight

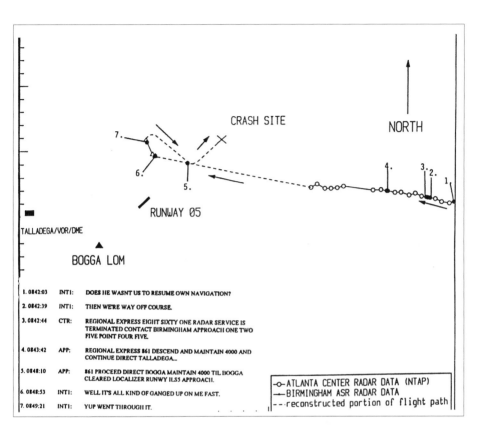

CRASH SITE

NORTH

7.

6.

5.

RUNWAY 05

TALLADEGA/VOR/DME

▲

BOGGA LOM

4.

3. 2.

1

1. 0842:03	INTI:	DOES HE WASNT US TO RESUME OWN NAVIGATION?
2. 0842:39	INTI:	THEN WE'RE WAY OFF COURSE.
3. 0842:44	CTR:	REGIONAL EXPRESS EIGHT SIXTY ONE RADAR SERVICE IS TERMINATED CONTACT BIRMINGHAM APPROACH ONE TWO FIVE POINT FOUR FIVE.
4. 0843:42	APP:	REGIONAL EXPRESS 861 DESCEND AND MAINTAIN 4000 AND CONTINUE DIRECT TALLADEGA...
5. 0848:10	APP:	861 PROCEED DIRECT BOGGA MAINTAIN 4000 TIL BOGGA CLEARED LOCALIZER RUNWY ILS5 APPROACH.
6. 0848:53	INTI:	WELL IT'S ALL KIND OF GANGED UP ON ME FAST.
7. 0849:21	INTI:	YUP WENT THROUGH IT.

—o—ATLANTA CENTER RADAR DATA (NTAP)
—•—BIRMINGHAM ASR RADAR DATA
- - -reconstructed portion of flight path

instructor for nine months before getting accepted by the commuter for training.

The captain had 857 hours of fixed-wing time when hired. He then went through the operator's ground and flight training program, which included 12.8 hours in the Beech 99 (including the initial qualification checkride).

The day of the accident was the first day of operation for the commuter's new southern route structure. It was also the captain's first day as an airline pilot and the regional chief pilot was supposed to be his first officer. However, maintenance problems with one of the commuter's airplanes required the regional chief pilot to ferry in a replacement airplane, so another first officer was called in.

The first officer on the accident flight had been flying the commuter's Midwest route for one month and had not flown the new route. Prior to getting hired, the first officer got most of his 1200 hours as a flight instructor.

Given the captain's lack of airline experience and given the first officer's recent-hire status, NTSB admonished the commuter for pairing these two pilots on the first day of a new route that neither pilot had flown previously. As a result, NTSB believed the pilots had insufficient experience in their roles as captain and first officer, which at times interfered with the safe conduct of the flight.

For example, you'll recall the captain asked the first officer whether they should maintain the 280° heading or intercept an airway. The first officer's reply was "280's fine because we're on course anyway..." which didn't give the captain the big picture about their route. Instead, the captain should have insisted that the first officer call ATC to confirm their routing.

The cockpit discussion indicated the captain was still confused about their position, which prompted him to further query the first officer. Again, the first officer's reply didn't clarify things when he told the captain the course was 085 inbound. He was describing the airway radial from TDG VOR, when instead he should have told the captain the inbound course was 265.

Bottom line: the first officer wasn't adequately assisting the captain in the management of the flight and the captain wasn't insistent enough to get the information he needed.

Crew Complexities

Multi-pilot crews are a way of life for commuter and air carrier operators. In addition, many pilots routinely fly IFR with a second pilot even though a second pilot isn't required under the rules of the flight. The essence of safe flight is for each crewmember to understand his/her role in the cockpit and to work together as a team, while all the time remembering there can only be one person in charge. This is why cockpit resource management (CRM) training was developed; to enhance the safety of multi-pilot operations.

You don't necessarily need a course in CRM just to fly IFR with a second pilot, but you do need a clear understanding of each person's duties and responsibilities during the flight. These responsibilities should be discussed before the flight.

Positional Awareness

There's no doubt the pilots of Flight 861 lost the picture of their position relative to the airport, the VOR and Bogga LOM. The first officer seemed convinced they were east of Bogga and when cleared for the approach believed they were at Bogga. Even if the crew had tracked the centerline of V-18, they would have flown over the airport and, at any given time, would have been northeast of Bogga. Their 280-heading put them north of the airway centerline, which meant they could only have been northeast of Bogga.

As stated earlier, there's no evidence the crew ever tuned and identified the LOM, which would have been a golden aid to positional awareness. There would have been little doubt about their position relative to Bogga and the entire approach had they used this navaid. When transitioning for and during an approach, use all available equipment to keep you oriented, e.g., ADF/RMI, DME, VOR cross-radial, etc.

The captain was confused for some time about their route and position and prompted the first officer several times to call ATC to find out. Instead of calling, the first officer tried to figure it out on his own. When they were cleared for the approach, even the first officer seemed confused.

When in doubt, ask ATC about your clearance, what route you're expected to fly and to confirm your position if necessary (that's what radar service is for). There was some question during the investigation as to whether the crew believed they were getting radar service during the approach.

Atlanta Center told Flight 861 "Radar service terminated, contact Birmingham Approach..." At this point, the crew should no longer have relied on radar vectors. When contacting Birmingham Approach, Flight 861 was told to descend to 4000 feet and to continue direct Talladega. This was a specific routing in which the crew should have expected to fly to TDG VOR, then via the 112-radial transition to Bogga.

Approach also told the crew if they couldn't get the airport in sight to expect the ILS from over Bogga. Flight 861 was told about weather southwest of Bogga and given a report that indicated the field was VFR. The crew completed the in-range checklist and the first officer said: Crew briefing, if we don't get the visual here in a few miles we'll do the ILS if we have to.

One minute later, the controller announced the new weather (which had deteriorated) and, shortly thereafter, instructed Flight 861 to proceed direct Bogga, maintain 4000 until Bogga, cleared ILS Runway 5. Again, a clearance for a specific route. If the crew had Bogga tuned in, all that was necessary was to fly direct to it and proceed outbound for the procedure turn.

During the investigation, it became apparent that the first officer believed they were getting vectors for either a visual approach or to Bogga IAF. The clearance issued by the approach controller did not in any way intimate the flight was getting vectors to Bogga. In fact, the last instruction by the controller was to advise procedure turn inbound. If the crew had called the controller when in doubt about their position relative to Bogga, they would have discovered they weren't in radar contact.

When getting vectors for an approach, a controller will state your position in relation to the fix in which you've been cleared, e.g., five miles south of Bogga. On the other hand, when you're cleared direct to a fix at a specific altitude without any position information, you must be able to navigate to the fix on your own. If you're confused about your position or how you're supposed to navigate to the fix, ask ATC. Get on a published route or to a fix at a safe altitude if necessary to sort things out.

Trusting Instincts

The captain remained confused about their position as he flew the approach and he also seemed to be uncomfortable about flying an unstabilized approach and the lack of a reliable glideslope indication. This uneasiness must have prompted him to say, We gotta go missed on this.

When an approach doesn't feel right and the situation doesn't appear to be under control, there's no loss of face in climbing to a safe altitude and reflying the approach with confidence. On the other hand, we all know what happens when we don't trust our instincts and press on regardless.

Section Five

Approach Accidents

Two Accidents at Gainesville

T here's nothing particularly unusual or hazardous about Gainesville Regional Airport, other than a cluster of television towers nearby. What makes this location of interest to us is that there were two IFR accidents there several years ago, both involving approaches.

These accidents could easily have fit into any of the other sections of this book; the causes were many and varied, ranging from engine failure to destabilized approaches to a loss of positional awareness to poor pilot judgment. We present them here as an illustration of the many things that can go wrong with an approach...and the many opportunities that pilots usually have to avert disaster.

Getting Into TV The Hard Way

The next time you hear of an airplane tangling with a TV tower surely won't be the first; especially when tall transmitters are located anywhere near an airport or flyway, it seems only a matter of time until someone manages to mix it up with the guy wires or the tower itself, almost always to the detriment of the aviator involved.

This is the story of a Twin Beech which tried to knock down a TV tower some years ago; the attempt was completely successful—the tower was flattened—but unfortunately, the pilot and his passengers also paid the big price. Perhaps even more than most aviation accidents, this one has a long, clear chain of events, any one of which might have stopped the mishap in its tracks.

Late October weather in north Florida is usually delightful. While the folks up north are resigning themselves to the onset of winter, Floridians are still basking in the warm sunshine. But every now and then, a slow-moving weather system covers most of the region with dense fog; it burns off by midday, but while it's dense, it's dense.

Such was the case on the morning our story begins. A small commercial operator in Tampa agreed to charter one of its Twin Beech airplanes to get a group together for a meeting in Lake City, 140 miles north. The pilot departed Tampa early in the morning with one passenger, picked up another in Bartow, then proceeded to Lake City.

So far, so good...but the weather didn't cooperate. The Lake City airport was fogged in to the tune of 400 overcast, visibility one and one half miles. Well, that's not quite true, because Lake City doesn't have a weather-reporting facility, and those were the conditions at Gainesville, some 35 miles to the south. With only a VOR approach, and an MDA of 660 feet, the chances of a successful approach at Lake City were pretty slim. Nevertheless, the pilot executed the procedure, and to no one's surprise, was forced to miss it.

Busted Regs

Something's wrong already. FAR Part 135 prohibits a for-hire flight from launching IFR to a destination with no weather-reporting service. And a pilot operating under Part 135 is specifically prohibited from commencing an instrument approach procedure unless he has a current report from the field that it is at or above minimums. Shouldn't the pilot wait for VFR conditions? He certainly should have, and the decision to start for Lake City may have forged the first link in the chain of events that led to the accident. But let's continue with the rest of the story.

Behind Schedule

By the time the abortive attempt to land at Lake City was over with, the folks in the back of the airplane were falling way behind schedule. The pilot headed for Gainesville at flank speed (in a Twin Beech that's not much), called ahead on unicom for a rental car, and prepared himself for a quick-and-dirty ILS to get his passengers on the ground ASAP. This may have been the second link in the accident chain..."The hurrier I go, the behinder I get."

We should share with you at this time something about the captain. An ex-Air Force pilot with more than 8,000 hours of flying time, he elected to remain in Tampa after retirement, and worked as a part-time charter pilot to stay active in aviation. From all appearances, including positive comments from his contemporaries, he was a professional in every sense of the word.

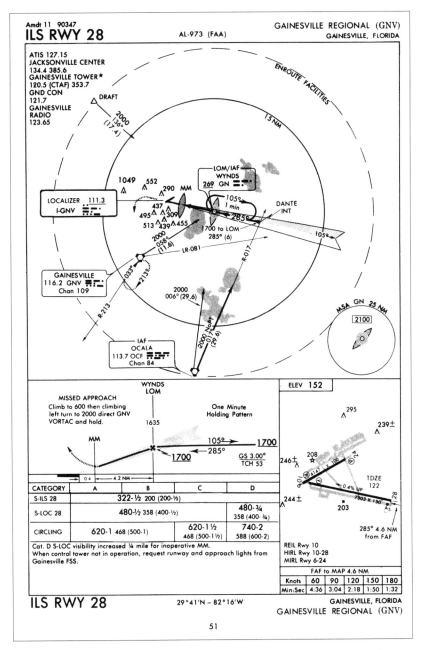

The forest of towers near the airport wasn't the problem...it was the tall one a few miles off the end of the runway.

Passenger Pressure?

So why did he start the day with a clear violation of the regulations? Is it possible that the perceived need to complete an assigned mission drove him to ignore the rules and press on? Did he permit pressure from schedule-conscious passengers to sway him from the sort of discipline he had surely learned in his military experience? We'll let you answer these questions for yourself. On with the story.

At Gainesville, Florida, the instrument runway is oriented east-west, with an ILS approach leading to runway 28 (see accompanying chart). A locator outer marker (LOM) is situated about five miles from the runway, the decision height is 200 feet above the touchdown zone, and the missed approach procedure requires a climb on the localizer to a safe altitude, followed by a turn to the holding fix.

A rather typical procedure, with one exception...about seven miles west of the airport, and almost directly on the centerline of the runway, is a group of TV towers, the tallest of which rises 869 feet above the ground. In all but the most extenuating circumstances, a pilot can count on the published missed approach procedure to provide a comfortable margin of clearance from the tower. As you'll see, the circumstances became very extenuating.

Trying to Make Time

When we left the Twin Beech, it was screaming toward the ILS at Gainesville, the pilot doing everything in his power for his passengers. About ten miles out, he was cleared to descend to procedure turn altitude, and cleared for the ILS approach. A post-accident radar plot revealed a groundspeed close to 200 knots during this portion of the approach, and that's moving for a Twin Beech.

A Hurried Procedure Turn

Four minutes after crossing the LOM outbound, the pilot reported over the marker inbound. Now four minutes is not a super-fast course reversal, but the radar record showed a wide, sweeping turn which suggested a tear-drop procedure, but which unfortunately overshot the localizer because of excessive speed. When the pilot called "marker inbound," he was actually a half-mile or so off to the side, and the aircraft was never stabilized on the approach from that point on. Gainesville tower was not equipped with radar at that time; the controllers accepted the report as accurate, and cleared the flight to land.

Two and a half minutes later, the pilot declared a missed approach, and was cleared to execute the published procedure, a climbing left turn to 2,000 feet and return to the VOR, east of the airport.

Why the missed approach? Gainesville weather at the time was 500 overcast, one and a half miles in fog, winds near-calm; conditions which should have been a piece of cake for this pilot, flying an airplane which could be flown at a very comfortable, slow airspeed on the approach.

But, you recall, radar showed an unstabilized localizer track, and apparently the pilot never got the glide path under control either. People located a half-mile north of the runway heard the airplane pass overhead, but no one saw it; it was still in the clouds, at least 300 feet above decision height.

The pilot had blown the approach, but at least he did the right thing and went around rather than try to salvage a bad situation.

Autopilot Inop

And now, a word about the airplane itself. This particular Twin Beech (Model E-18S) was built in 1956, but that doesn't make it all bad; there are lots of these old-timers still flying all over the world. They require lots of care, and the maintenance records of this E-18S left some doubt in investigators' minds about the overall condition of the airplane. There were several outstanding discrepancies, the most glaring of which was an inoperative autopilot; it had been on the fritz for some time before the accident, and this situation was known to the mechanics, the dispatchers and the pilot.

Isn't there something in FAR Part 135 that speaks to single-pilot IFR with an autopilot in lieu of a second-in-command?

Sure is, and as you might expect, it says that a qualified pilot may operate an airplane like this IFR all by himself, as long as he has the help of an autopilot. Of course, the autopilot must be working. Another link in the chain.

I've Got a Little Trouble Here

At this point, the luck which had seen the pilot through an illegal IFR flight, an aborted VOR approach and a botched ILS, began to drain away. When the pilot didn't respond to the missed approach instructions, the controller asked, "Did you copy, sir?" The pilot responded, "Ah roger, I've got a little trouble here." On further inquiry, the controller found out that the Twin Beech was now a Single Beech...the right engine had failed.

"Six five Victor, if you're receiving Wynds (the LOM) you can proceed back to Wynds via direct, maintain two thousand if able sir, and you are cleared for the ILS runway two eight approach." No response. "Six five Victor, Gainesville Tower."

And finally, a response: "Six five Victor, I'm still with you, but I'm having trouble getting the engine feathered."

This pilot was in serious trouble. Even with a light load, the Twin Beech is not a skyrocket on one engine...to say nothing of the enormous drag generated by a windmilling propeller.

Witnesses located in the accident area seven miles west of the airport observed the airplane flying just beneath the clouds. They saw it roll sharply to the right and dive for the ground just before the right wing caught one of the guy wires on the TV tower. The pilot and all of his passengers died in the crash and fire which followed.

No Single Engine Climb

It was obvious that the cause of the crash was the inability of the airplane to climb with a failed engine and windmilling propeller, and there was no doubt that the pilot was unable to turn the airplane to the left, as the missed approach procedure instructed. But investigators were intrigued by the sharp roll and dive reported by witnesses just before collision with the guy wire. A near-identical airplane was acquired for a series of flight tests in an attempt to recreate the situation. A missed approach was initiated 200 feet above DH, and power on the right engine was reduced.

The pilot of the test airplane was a highly experienced former military multi-engine pilot, with a great deal of time in light twins. Despite knowing exactly what to expect, and despite the advantage of conducting the test in clear weather, this veteran pilot was unable to make the Twin Beech turn to the left, and could not coax it any higher than 700 feet agl...the highest altitude observed on radar just before the crash.

It is highly unlikely that the pilot of the accident airplane could have remained airborne much longer, and the eyewitness reports strongly suggest that aircraft control was lost coincidentally with the wire strike. We are taught in multi-engine training that airplanes will not climb at Vmc; it's an airspeed to be avoided at all costs.

But when you are close to the ground, flying a severely crippled airplane in solid clouds, the instinctive reaction is to climb...and the only recourse is to raise the pitch attitude. During the post-accident flight tests, the airplane was shuddering on the verge of a stall through- out the attempted climb, and at 700 feet, density altitude defeated any further vertical progress. It would have taken a lot of intestinal fortitude and huge doses of self-discipline to the airplane straight ahead into the ground, hoping for the best.

There are several lessons to be learned from this accident: first, don't break the rules, no matter which part of the FARs you're working under; second, don't let someone else's schedule (or your own, for that matter) push you into a hurry-up IFR procedure; and third, if you find yourself at the controls of a multi-engine airplane with an engine out and a failed feathering system, be sure that your religious connections are intact.

This accident has a couple of notable similarities to the last one. It, too, happened as the result of a botched ILS 28 approach at Gainesville. It's evident that the approach was botched because the pilot was in a hurry, and didn't take the time to make sure the thing was done right.

Not *Another* One

The following conversation took place several years ago between a controller in the tower at Gainesville, Florida and one of his counterparts in Jacksonville Center:

Tower: It looks like we got one down. We got a call from the fire department and they are responding to a report of a plane crash out west of the airport, out near the towers out there.
Center: Okay, I understand. We have another airplane holding east of the marker waiting for clearance to land.
Tower: Okay, they are going to call us back as soon as they verify the report.(Five minutes later)
Tower: Okay, Center, we definitely have a crash. They haven't been able to verify the tail number, but he apparently hit the antennas out west of the airport.
Center: Oh boy, again?
Tower: Again.
Center: Is that the one they just rebuilt, the one the other twin Beech hit?
Tower: It's the same area. I don't know if he hit the same antenna or not, but it might be a good possibility. He is down and I guess you are going to need a tail number before you can clear anybody else for the approach.
Center: Okay, when you find out, let us know.

No wonder the controllers were surprised. It isn't often that two airplanes manage to collide with a ground obstruction in near-identical conditions in a relatively short period of time.

Even though there are striking similarities, this accident is slightly different. There is, however, a strong thread of commonalty; a procedural problem, which runs throughout this episode. See if you can figure out what it is.

VFR at First

The Baron was commanded by a 47-year old, 3000-hour pilot, a school principal who flew for a corporation on a part-time basis. He departed a small airport in West Virginia and headed for Florida. Although the Gainesville weather on this October day was IFR (400 overcast and one mile at the time of the accident), the pilot elected to forego a weather briefing (at least there is no record of his contacting any briefing facility before takeoff). We must assume that he was able to climb VFR to 8500 feet and remain in VFR conditions during the initial part of the flight.

At 11:30 that morning (in the vicinity of Alma, Georgia), Baron N4158S called Jacksonville Center and requested VFR advisories. Following the establishment of radar contact, N58S was silent for eight minutes; the reason was clear when the pilot called Center again:

N58S: Baron Four-One-Five-Eight-Sierra, we just dropped off to get a weather briefing for Gainesville. Looks like we're gonna have to pick up an IFR to get in there. Ah, can we go direct with you IFR, or do I need to go back and file?
Center: Ah negative, we'll take it here on the frequency. Be advised I've lost radar contact with you. I should pick you up just around Baxley Intersection and I'll have an IFR for you there.

Ten minutes passed and the Baron came into radar range. After some discussion:

Center: Four-One-Five-Eight-Sierra, I have you in radar contact. You are cleared to the Gainesville Airport via direct Taylor [VOR], Victor 157 Gainesville, maintain niner thousand.
N58S: Five-Eight-Sugar, roger, we'll level at nine and we're cleared ah to Taylor ah to Gainesville via the airway.
Center: Five-Eight-Sierra, readback is correct, Alma altimeter 30.14.

Well, the readback was mostly correct. There was lots of room for improvement, but the pilot apparently had the important parts in mind. Shortly thereafter, N58S was handed off to the next Jacksonville Center sector, and eleven minutes later, was cleared to descend to 7000 feet.

At this point, let's review the land-line communications between Center and the controller in Gainesville Tower. It's important to understand that when an IFR flight is transferred from one controller to another, certain information is passed along:

Center: Gainesville, I've got two estimates.
Tower: Okay, go ahead.
Center: The first one is Four-Seven-Seven-Whiskey, a BE 58, estimating Wynds at ah one six two eight, ILS Runway 28. The next one is ah Four-One-Five-Eight-Sierra, also a BE 58, Wynds at one six three one, ILS Runway 28.

Notice that there are two Beech Barons inbound to Gainesville (Wynds is the LOM for the ILS 28 approach), with N58S running three minutes behind the other airplane. N58S by this time had passed Taylor, and was well on its way towards Gainesville. At this point, refer to the accompanying reproduction of the Baron's radar track. The pilot is about to pass Point#4 on the diagram.

Center: Four-One-Five-Eight-Sierra, you're cleared direct Wynds, fly heading one-three-zero until able to navigate direct. (Point #4)
N58S: Five-Eight-Sugar, roger sir, cleared direct Wynds. Ah reading ah Wynds ah navigational steady now.
Center: Four-One-Five-Eight-Sierra, descend and maintain four thousand.
N58S: Five-Eight-Sierra, leaving seven for four.

Notice that the heading from the Baron to Wynds was about 130°; the pilot was going to have to turn 150° to get onto the localizer, which, naturally, calls for a procedure turn unless the controller issues vectors to get the airplane more-or-less lined up with the final approach course. (You can see it coming, can't you?)
  At about this time, the controller apparently noticed that the actual positions of the two Barons approaching Gainesville were slightly different than the original estimates and he offered N58S an opportunity to take the lead:

Center: Five-Eight-Sierra, can you give me a little better rate of descent? I'll be able to get you in first.
N58S: Five-Eight-Sugar, roger, we'll drop it out.
Center: Four-One-Five-Eight-Sierra, roger, descend and maintain two thousand. (Point #5)
N58S: Five-Eight-Sugar, roger sir, down to two.

Just how much of a descent rate is meant by "we'll drop it out" is open

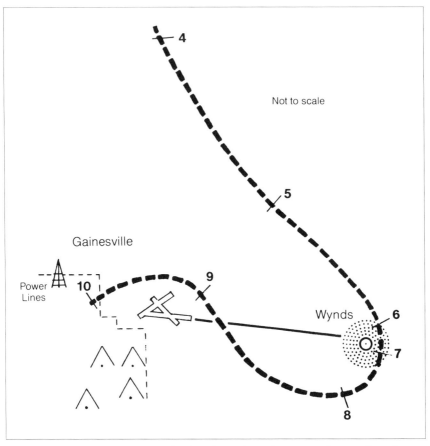

to interpretation, but it undoubtedly referred to something other than a normal descent to approach altitude. Since N58S reported level at 2000 feet four minutes later, his average rate of descent must have been 1250 feet per minute; certainly not excessive, but faster than usual. It's likely that airspeed also increased during the descent.

The Center controller also advised Gainesville Tower of the change in sequence:

Center: Gainesville Tower, reference ah Four-One-Five-Eight- Sierra and Seven-Seven-Whiskey.
Tower: Go ahead.Center: Okay, Five-Eight-Sierra is gonna be number one. Make him at the Wynds beacon at ah two eight and make ah Seven-Seven- Whiskey at three one.
Tower: Okay.

We move ahead a few minutes. Five-Eight Sierra has just reached 2000, is probably moving fairly fast, and is almost on top of Wynds LOM. Not to mention that the Baron is moving in a southerly direction, roughly 90 degrees to the final approach course:

N58S: Five-Eight-Sierra level at two thousand.
Center: Five-Eight-Sierra, roger, cleared for an ILS approach Runway 28 at Gainesville. (Point #6)
N58S: Five-Eight-Sugar, roger sir, understand cleared for the approach.
Center: Four-One-Five-Eight-Sierra, roger, I have you over Wynds radio beacon. Contact Gainesville Tower 120.5.
N58S: Five-Eight-Sugar. (Point #7)

After about thirty seconds, Five-Eight-Sierra checked in with the tower:

N58S: Gainesville Tower, Baron Four-One-Five-Eight-Sierra with you, ah, ah picking up the localizer. (Point #8—Note that at this point the approach is essentially blown.)
Tower: Baron Four-One-Five-Eight-Sierra, Gainesville Tower, report the Wynds outer compass locator inbound.
N58S: Say again?
Tower: Baron Four-One-Five-Eight-Sierra, report the Wynds outer compass locator inbound.
N58S: Five-Eight-Sugar.

Two and one-half minutes after his initial contact with tower, the pilot of the Baron reported as instructed:

N58S: Five-Eight-Sierra, ah at the outer marker. (Point #9)
Tower: Baron Four-One-Five-Eight-Sierra, cleared to land runway 28, wind is 030 at five.
N58S: Five-Eight-Sugar.

Definitely Disoriented

That was the last transmission from N58S. Let's back up to the point where the pilot was handed off to the tower. As we noted above, he had just completed a descent and was virtually on top of the LOM traveling at right angles to the localizer. Instead of turning outbound when cleared for the approach, the pilot turned westbound, towards the airport. By the time he contacted the tower, the pilot was well southwest of the LOM, and far off the localizer. He'd blown the approach already, but apparently didn't know it. Based on the subsequent transmissions, he didn't seem to realize that he had already passed Wynds.

When the pilot reported at the outer marker, the airplane was abeam the end of the runway, well off the localizer and certainly nowhere near the outer marker. Did he mistake the middle marker signals for the outer marker? Did he really believe that he was still east of the outer marker? Of course, we'll never really know what the pilot thought, but it's clear that he was badly confused. How could a routine ILS approach go so wrong, on a day with almost no wind and a ceiling/visibility combination that should have provided visual contact with the runway?

The answer to that question involves a number of considerations: positional awareness, aircraft control, knowledge of IFR procedures, good judgment, eagerness to get on the ground and perhaps misinterpretation of ATC instructions.

On the latter count, the lawsuit that resulted from this accident took the controllers to task for not monitoring the airplane's flight path and advising the pilot that he was way off course. We're going to set that aside for this discussion, so we can concentrate on what the pilot should have done, but there is at least one observation to be made with regard to the pilot-controller relationship; no matter what ATC says, the pilot remains responsible for the safe conduct of the flight. It is possible that the pilot was so accustomed to radar vectors to the final approach course, that he considered himself on such a vector in this instance. Even if that were true, a red flag should have leaped into the pilot's mind when the controller advised, "I have you over the Wynds radio beacon at this time."

It would take some kind of piloting skills to bend a Baron around 180-plus degrees of turn at the outer marker, then turn 90 degrees in the opposite direction in order to stay on the localizer, all the while getting the airplane configured for the approach and descending on the glideslope. That maneuver would be impossible.

How about positional awareness? Shouldn't the pilot have planned a course reversal outside the marker and shouldn't he have been aware of his direct course to Wynds? It seems that the controller's announcement "I have you over the Wynds radio beacon at this time" should have served as a welcome confirmation of where the airplane was located.

An instrument pilot should not execute a procedure turn (course reversal) given any of the following: when cleared straight in, when radar vectored to the final approach course, or when the chart clearly indicates (NoPT) that a procedure turn is not required. None of these conditions applied in this situation.

So, we're down to good judgment and eagerness to get on the ground. True, the pilot was offered an inducement to speed up the procedure. Who among us is not sorely tempted to accept such an offer? But the controller's inquiry, "Four-One-Five-Eight-Sierra, can you give me a little better rate of descent? I'll be able to get you in first" related only to expediting the approach to the marker, not short-cutting the procedure itself. There was no mention in the clearance of a vector to the final approach course. It was reasonable for the controller to assume that the Baron would proceed outbound, get turned around and fly the ILS in a normal fashion.

In his apparent eagerness to get the airplane on the ground, this pilot attempted what was surely impossible. Complete disorientation occurred and the airplane was at a very low altitude, completely outside the envelope of any of the navaids being used. It is obvious that the pilot was very confused. The only remedy in that set of circumstances (no runway in sight, needles not where they belong, time has run out, not sure of position) is an immediate missed approach.

Fly Stabilized Approaches

All of these considerations (awareness, control, knowledge, judgment) fit into a neat operational package that will forestall such an unhappy event in almost every case: fly stabilized approaches. Especially when you are approaching a strange airport, when the weather is down and it's important to complete the approach procedure the first time. Get your airplane slowed down, properly configured, properly positioned and don't descend until you are satisfied that all you'll have to do in the final stages of the procedure is maintain control and look for the runway. By "final stages" we mean from the time you interecept the glideslope (*already* established on the localizer) until you either break out or execute the missed approach.

Think about it: That means that you must have all your ducks in a row, with a very clear idea of where you are and what you're doing, well before you're cleared for the approach. The pilot of N4158S obviously did not have that degree of positional and situational awareness when he flew over the LOM.

We didn't mention it by its most familiar name, but get-there-itis can be just as deadly as get-home-itis. In closing, consider Murphy's Third Law of Instrument Approaches: If it doesn't look right and if it doesn't feel right, it probably isn't.

Deciding
To Miss

For most of us, most approaches are successful on the first try. Occasionally it's obvious that the approach just won't work, and we either call it quits and divert or try one before heading for the alternate.

Every once in a while, though, the weather is hovering right around minimums. You might be able to make it...you try, and miss. What now? Try again? If so, how many times? What other factors are there? How much of a problem would it be for you to land elsewhere?

The urge to get on the ground, on time, and at your intended destination can be overwhelming. So overwhelming, in fact, that it proved the undoing of the pilot in this case.

If at First....

The runway acts like a magnet for some instrument pilots; regardless of the conditions, they will try to get the airplane on the ground no matter what. In a highly publicized air carrier accident a few years ago, a DC-9 flew into a downburst as it crossed the middle marker during an ILS approach. During the attempted go-around, the captain spotted the runway and elected to land instead of continuing the missed approach. The airplane slammed onto the runway, sheared the gear and slid to a stop with few injuries but major airframe damage.

Getting onto the runway is the ultimate objective of any flight, but there are times when it's better to do something else...with the almost-always-available alternative of coming back for another try under better conditions.

In this case, a long series of events and circumstances connected a normal takeoff and a catastrophic accident, with the pilot's repeated attempts to get on the ground playing the leading role. Perhaps the easiest way to study the anatomy of this accident is to consider those areas which are part and parcel of every instrument flight: the machine, the environment, the facilities and the man.

The Machine

N174YC was an old Beech 18 (there aren't any new ones), one of those sturdy birds that just keeps on flying. It was owned by the pilot, and as far as investigators could determine, had been inspected and maintained in complete accordance with applicable FARs. This Twin Beech had a complete set of flight instruments on each side of the panel, one air driven, the other electrical. It was loaded with full fuel (1548 pounds), seven people and all the gear from a just-completed fishing trip. Investigators calculated that the airplane was about 300 pounds over maximum gross weight at takeoff.

The Environment

The pilot received a weather briefing for the Chicago area prior to filing an IFR flight plan from International Falls, Minnesota to DuPage County Airport, about 15 miles southwest of Chicago O'Hare. The proposed time en route was three hours and thirty minutes. The briefing was obtained well in advance of the 6:30 pm takeoff and included the 5:00 pm sequence reports for DuPage (estimated 1800 broken, 10,000 overcast, four miles in haze) and O'Hare (1600 scattered, 3000 scattered, estimated 25,000 broken, five miles in haze).

Terminal forecasts indicated 1000 scattered, 2000 broken, four miles in haze (scattered variable to broken) until 11:00 pm, then 1000 overcast, three miles in fog variable to 500 overcast, one mile in fog. The forecasts that were issued to the pilot did not accurately depict the ceiling and visibility that existed at the time of the accident, but amendments issued after the briefing were substantially accurate. As we'll see, the pilot received several reports of worse than forecast weather.

Lowering ceilings and visibility west of Chicago that night should not have been a surprise with the temperature and dew point close and a light northeasterly wind blowing off Lake Michigan, which carried lake moisture over the cooler land.

A routine observation 28 minutes prior to the accident showed that the DuPage weather deteriorated to an indefinite ceiling of 400 sky obscured, visibility two and one-half miles in fog and haze, temperature 58, dew point 56, wind 060 at 11. Eight minutes after the accident, a special observation reported an indefinite ceiling of 100 sky obscured, visibility one mile in fog.

The Facilities

For an instrument pilot at the time of this accident, DuPage County Airport was a one-runway facility, with VOR and localizer procedures to runway 10. The runway was 4000 feet long, 75 feet wide and equipped with medium intensity runway lights (MIRL), runway end identification lights (REIL) and runway alignment indicator lights (RAIL). The only lighting available when the pilot flew this procedure was the MIRL since all the other lights were controlled by tower personnel and the tower closed at 10:00 pm, just prior to the Twin Beech's last approach.

Since the pilot selected the localizer approach, let's review the numbers for that procedure; final approach fix located so as to provide sufficient time to descend to the MDA in order to spot the runway, an MDA of 1180 feet msl (424 feet agl) and a missed approach procedure which called for a climb and a right turn to the Joliet vortac. The circling MDA was considerably higher, well into the clouds on the night of this accident.

The Man

Based on his records, the 34-year old pilot started flying relatively late in life, but appeared to be very ambitious and sincerely interested in aviation. Once under way, he earned his private pilot certificate in two and one-half months, a commercial certificate one year later, a multi-engine rating a year after that and a flight instructor certificate the following year. He continued and obtained a helicopter rating two months before the accident.

The pilot's total time was approximately 920 hours. His log indicated 328 hours of multi-engine, the majority of it in the Piper Aztec. He flew the Twin Beech a total of 43 hours (11 dual), of which only 1.6 hours were in actual weather, 0.6 under the hood and 4.3 hours at night. A lot of experienced pilots will agree that it takes more time than that to develop the feel for an airplane, more time than that to generate the confidence in yourself and the machine that will enable you to perform well in adverse conditions and circumstances.

Of even more significance to the analysis of this accident is the fact that the pilot was not IFR current. He logged only three hours of instrument time in the previous six months and only four approaches. His logbook indicated that the last time he was IFR current was five months ago and that he flew several times in violation of FAR 61.57. Some pilots can remain reasonably proficient with less than the pre-scribed experience minimums, but perhaps the willingness to fly in violation of these basic regulations may be indicative of a willingness to take unnecessary risks in other areas as well.

The Accident

N174YC departed International Falls at 6:44 pm, 465 miles and nearly three and one-half hours away from Chicago. Unfortunately, we don't have the benefit of a communication transcript to capture all the details of the flight, but the information available helps reconstruct what took place.

The Twin Beech climbed to 9000 feet, where it remained for one hour and twenty minutes. ATC then cleared the flight to 10,000 feet to resolve a traffic conflict. One hour later, N74YC was cleared to 7000 feet as the first step of the approach to DuPage County Airport. Would two-plus hours at 10,000 feet affect the pilot's judgment? It's impossible to say for sure, but each of us reacts differently to high-altitude exposure and even a bit of hypoxia could have figured in this accident.

To his credit, the pilot checked on the DuPage weather as the flight progressed. At 9:15 pm, the Center controller provided N74YC with the most recent observation: sky partially obscured, ceiling 25,000 overcast, visibility two and one-half miles in fog. Twenty-five minutes later, the pilot inquired again, and was advised that a special observation made just ten minutes after the previous report showed an indefinite ceiling of 700 feet sky obscured, visibility one mile in fog and haze.

These reports were quite a change from the weather that was forecast and there were a couple of warning flags flying. First, a special weather observation is taken only when there is a significant change in conditions, primarily in ceiling and/or visibility...a pilot's thinking should be heading toward Plan B when hearing a special observation at destination.

Second, an obscuration, either partial or complete, is a unique phenomenon. It's officially described as a ground-based condition which prevents the observer from seeing the sky condition itself. From the pilot's perspective, an obscuration should raise the immediate question of the ability to see the runway when breaking out of the clouds. In a normal situation (a ceiling with no obscuration), you can usually count on good slant range visibility as you descend below the cloud layer which forms the ceiling. In this case, the sky was obscured by fog and haze which started at ground level, and slant range visibility was severely reduced.

Two events occurred which may have led the pilot deeper into a questionable weather situation. The DuPage ATIS reported a ceiling of 400 feet overcast and a visibility of two and one-half miles. The tower advised N74YC that another pilot had reported the ceiling at 400 feet, which was the MDA for the localizer approach.

We need to consider the Twin Beech's fuel state at this point. The two Pratt & Whitney 985 engines each consume about 40 gallons per hour. With 258 gallons at takeoff, N74YC was pressing its reserve on a three and one-half hour flight. No alternate was filed (although one was clearly required) and the nearest reasonable airport away from the wind-induced fog was approximately 40 miles to the west. The pilot was surely aware of his fuel situation and may have felt compelled to proceed straight to DuPage and land on the first approach...a dangerous situation and a dangerous state of mind.

The first attempt started with problems. The controller noticed that the airplane was aligned well south of the localizer, advised the pilot and offered a choice of vectors to intercept the course or start the approach all over again. The pilot elected to intercept, and shortly thereafter, reported that he lost his localizer, followed in quick succession with, "My gyros went out, I'm flying with the instruments on the right side."

This is a grim situation for any pilot and one that should generate thoughts about going elsewhere. The pilot of N74YC persisted, however; he reported that his instruments were back and requested vectors for another localizer approach. When the time came to be handed-off to the tower, he was advised to contact the DuPage Flight Service Station, since the tower was closed. This meant that the approach light systems were also shut down. (More warning flags.)

The pilot reported runway in sight at 1012:15 and directly overhead a minute and a half later. He also said that it looked clearer to the north, and that he would try to circle left and land. That didn't work out and the next communication from N74YC indicated that the pilot once again had the runway in sight, and intended to circle to the right and land on runway 28.

A witness on the airport saw and heard all of the attempts to land. He said that the airplane was directly over and almost halfway down the runway when it broke out of the fog, which he estimated at 300 to 400 feet above the ground. The pilot added power and circled to the left. He came back over the airport again but did not align with the runway in sufficient time to land. He then circled to the left again, this time going further west before returning to the airport. "The third and last time I saw the plane he was directly over the runway and this time he was far enough down that I figured he had it made. But instead of landing, he went past the tower, added power and banked hard to the right in a climbing attitude," the witness said.

That's a lot of maneuvering at night, at low altitude, in low visibility and perhaps using instruments on the other side of the panel. Immediately after his last pass across the runway, the pilot reported to the FSS that he lost ground contact and that he was going back to the VOR. He then asked about the weather at other Chicago area airports and his final words were "How about a radar vec...." N74YC slammed into a corn field south of the airport in a 40-degree nose-down attitude, with absolutely no forward movement after impact.

The Questions

What caused this accident? Spatial disorientation, without a doubt. In addition to all the maneuvering, the strong possibility that the pilot was using the right-side instruments and the lack of visual cues on the ground, consider that investigators determined that the landing lights were illuminated at impact. Have you ever flown in solid clouds with the lights on? If you try it, be sure you have plenty of altitude. There are many illusions in this situation.

Should this flight have been attempted? There appears to be no reason why not, but there were several points along the way when an alternate plan should have been considered. This assumes, of course, that the pilot had no prior knowledge of instrument and avionics problems with the airplane. Going into an approach procedure with the weather at minimums with known instrumentation problems is shaky at best.

Was this pilot predisposed to land at DuPage that night, no matter what? Probably, when one considers the fuel situation, the failure to file an alternate and, most significantly, his decision-making and his actions following the discovery that the instruments and avionics were behaving in less than an acceptable manner. Two attempts at a circling maneuver below the circling MDA at night in low visibility indicates a firm resolve to get on the ground.

Should the tower controller have remained at his post during the Twin Beech's approach? The obvious consideration is whether the complete approach lighting system would have made a difference in the outcome and that will never be answered...maybe yes, maybe no. On the other hand, the controller is certainly entitled to close up and go home when quitting time comes around. If the pilot had done his homework, he would have known that the approach light systems were not available after the tower closed for the night.

Should a missed approach procedure be continued once initiated? In almost every case, yes. There are times when a pilot can change his mind without compromising safety, but usually the conditions that prompted the missed approach are sufficient to dictate a continuation of the procedure, as published.

The Conclusion

It's so simple we tend to ignore it...Plan your flight and fly your plan. That time-worn reminder will always work, especially if the planning portion includes a complete familiarization with all of the information bearing on a proposed flight, and if the flying portion isn't so rigid that it doesn't permit any flexibility once the flight is under way.

When things in aviation don't look right, don't feel right, they probably aren't right. Start searching for the reasons and be prepared to execute Plan B.

Preconceived Ideas

*I*f you were being vectored for an ILS approach with the weather reported at minimums, would you expect to see the lights when reaching decision height? How would you mentally prepare yourself to fly the approach? The answers to these questions might have been important factors for the two pilots in this accident. They were flying an Embraer Bandeirante (a twin-engine turboprop commuter) on a scheduled run from Detroit to Alpena, MI with seven passengers.

As we noted in the last volume of the Instrument Pilot's Library, it's a good idea to fly every approach with the full expectation that you'll have to execute the missed. A great many approach accidents could have been avoided had the pilot simply shoved the throttles in and called it quits in time.

Great Expectations

The two pilots entered their company's operations office at Detroit Metropolitan Airport (DTW) at three o'clock on a snowy March afternoon. Many of this commuter's flights were either severely delayed or canceled that day due to weather. As a result, the crew didn't depart on their first flight until six o'clock, a round-trip to Toledo, OH of approximately one hour. They returned to Detroit with the DME inoperative.

The next scheduled flight for the crew was scrubbed when their destination went below minimums. Finally, the two pilots were assigned Flight 1746 to Alpena, which departed Detroit at 8:50 p.m. with the DME still inop.

At 9:25 p.m., while being vectored to the ILS Runway 1, Flight 1746 got the following Alpena weather from Wurtsmith Approach: sky partially obscured, measured ceiling 100 overcast, visibility one-half mile, light drizzle, fog, temperature 33° F, dew point 33° F, wind 110° at seven knots with fog obscuring nine-tenths of the sky.

The standard procedure for relaying weather to the commuter flights was for the National Weather Service (NWS) observer at Alpena to report to the Pellston, MI FSS, who then provided it to Wurtsmith Approach. As you might imagine, this procedure could result in a delay in getting the most current weather to the pilot during rapidly changing conditions, which is exactly what happened in this case.

The weather given Flight 1746 was reported at 8:50 p.m. A special observation was made at 9:19 p.m. when the visibility deteriorated to 3/8 mile, which put the field below minimums. This latest change, however, wasn't passed along to the crew. According to FAR 135, under which the flight was operated, the crew wasn't allowed to start the approach once the visibility fell below minimums.

At 9:33 p.m., Flight 1746 was 15 miles south-southwest of Felps LOM, given a heading of 25° to intercept the localizer and cleared for the approach. The crew then called the company station manager at Alpena and told him they'd be on the ground in five minutes. The station manager (who often relayed current weather), wasn't aware the visibility had gone below one-half mile. No weather was available from Alpena Tower either, since it was already closed for the day.

Even though the crew wasn't aware the visibility had dropped, they shouldn't have been hopeful about seeing anything at DH due to the marginal conditions.

Nine minutes later, the crew told Wurtsmith they had missed the approach and wanted vectors for another shot at it. The controller told 1746 to maintain 2800 feet and to proceed direct to Felps LOM. The flight was then cleared for another ILS.

As they flew the missed approach, the station manager went outside the terminal and heard the airplane overhead the field, but he couldn't see it. The crew then called and asked him to verify if the runway lights were on their highest level. He checked and responded that the lights were on full intensity.

Meanwhile, the NWS specialist made another observation since the visibility had dropped to one-quarter mile. The specialist immediately told the station manager, who tried to relay the new weather to the crew, but they had already left the frequency.

Crew Disoriented?

Several minutes passed, then the following exchange took place, indicating that the crew was uncertain of their position:

1746: Seventeen Forty-Six, can you give us some vectors back to the (unintelligible) procedure turn?
Approach: Seventeen Forty-Six, be advised you're too low for radar identification. If you'd want it, climb and maintain 4000.
1746: Okay, we're out of three for four, Seventeen Forty-Six.
Approach: Seventeen Forty-Six, say your position now.
1746: Okay, we're negative DME. We're going outbound 150.

The controller acknowledged and asked the crew to report reaching 4000 feet, which they did. Flight 1746 was picked up on radar one mile southeast of the Alpena Vortac and told to fly 160° for another ILS. During the vectors that followed, the controller (unaware of the latest visibility) asked the crew about the conditions during their first approach. "We picked up the lights, but we were in a little bit...but I'm not really sure what the visibility was and you know there's just fog, it was really hard to tell," said the first officer.

At 9:53, Flight 1746 was five miles from Felps and told to turn right heading 350, maintain at or above 2800 till established on the localizer, cleared ILS Runway 1. One and a half minutes later:

Approach: Seventeen Forty-Six, are you established on approach?
1746: Negative.

The controller told the flight to report established on the localizer, which was acknowledged. Then,

Approach: Seventeen Forty-Six, verify you are on the localizer. (There was no response, so the controller repeated the request.)
1746: That's affirm.
Approach: Seventeen Forty-Six, radar service terminated. Report your down time via this frequency, change to advisory frequency approved.

The crew acknowledged this instruction and wasn't heard from again. The airplane crashed in a wooded area one and a half miles south of the runway and 300 feet left of the localizer centerline. Two passengers managed to get out of the wreckage and walk to a nearby road, where they flagged down a motorist. The captain and five passengers survived.

Difficult Investigation

Reconstructing the events leading to this accident was extremely difficult for several reasons. First, the airplane wasn't equipped with (nor was it required to have) a cockpit voice or flight data recorder. Second, the Wurtsmith Air Force Base radar facility that handled the flight didn't have the equipment to record the airplane's ground track and altitude data. Finally, due to injuries sustained in the crash, the captain wasn't able to recall the accident in detail.

Despite the lack of detailed information, it seems clear that the crew's decisions and lack of positional awareness affected the outcome of the flight. Without knowing the visibility was reported below minimums during the first approach, the crew responded appropriately by executing a missed approach. During its investigation, NTSB asked the captain why he attempted a second approach. "Because we may have seen the lights on the first one, and we were still given half a mile as to current weather, because we were going to go around and try it again," was his response.

So it seems the crew caught a glimpse of either the approach or runway lights on the go-around and got sucked into believing they could make it on a second pass. This undoubtedly prompted the pilots' call to ask if the lights were at full intensity. They could have also asked for updated weather, since the NWS specialist's office was only 50 feet from the station manager.

Even if the crew believed the visibility was still a half mile, there's a big difference between what you can see straight down vs. on an angle from the cockpit. The go-around should have reinforced that, especially since they were in light drizzle and fog with no temperature/dew point spread; a condition that makes slant visibility next to zero.

If you've never tried it, have a flight instructor accompany you on a low-visibility approach in fog, assuming that it can be done safely. You'll be amazed how well you can see straight down, to the point where you'll probably see the approach lights and even the runway. But when you descend into and try to look at an angle through the fog, you'll be lucky to see past the front cowling. Seeing the runway straight down has suckered many a pilot into believing he or she can make it by flying successive approaches while going lower on each approach until finding the runway or, tragically, the ground.

In 1986, the pilot of a light twin tried to land at Tampa, FL with a visibility of one-sixteenth mile in fog. During his second ILS approach, the pilot collided with a B-727 that was holding short of the runway. When the temperature and dew point meet in stable conditions, probably nothing will change dramatically in the time it takes to fly another approach.

In the case of Flight 1746, the crew could have continued to their next destination (80 miles northwest), where the weather was one thousand

and three. Sure, the passengers who wanted to be in Alpena that night would've been unhappy, but that's a small price to pay for safety.

Positional Awareness

The conversations between Flight 1746 and ATC following the missed approach indicates the crew was confused about their position. This might be due to the fact that the DME wasn't working that night. With the Alpena Vortac right on the field, the crew would've had good distance information, even though the 7.3 DME fix at Felps wasn't established at the time of the accident.

Flight 1746's clearance was straightforward, Climb and maintain 2800, proceed direct Felps LOM. So why did the crew ask to be vectored? The most likely answer was discovered the next morning when FAA technicians arrived and found the Felps LOM out of service. This navaid wasn't monitored by any ATC facility, so no one except the pilots could have known whether it was functioning.

This situation is one good reason why you should always positively identify every navaid you intend to use. It's a good idea to keep the ident volume of a navaid you're using for an approach at a sufficient level so you can tell if it fails.

No Problems Expressed

It's interesting that the crew of Flight 1746 never mentioned any problems receiving the LOM. Their first approach probably wasn't affected by this problem, since they got a 20-degree intercept angle to the localizer 15 miles outside Felps. The crew was undoubtedly able to identify Felps with their marker beacon receiver as a result.

The circumstances of the second approach were altogether different. We can only speculate that they might have gotten confused while trying to tune the LOM and discovered they couldn't navigate to it. If this was the case, they should have told the controller. Without the LOM, the crew would've needed alternate missed approach instructions, since the missed approach holding pattern was at Felps and the minimum safe altitude was also based on this facility.

There was additional guidance for navigating to Felps. The chart shows a transition from the vortac out the 188 radial at 2800 feet and 7.3 miles to Felps. The crew might not have been comfortable doing this without DME and asked to be vectored instead.

Explain Your Predicament

When in doubt, there's nothing wrong with asking ATC for assistance.

When asking, though, you should explain your predicament, e.g., Excuse me, ATC, but my DME isn't working and I'm not receiving the LOM. How about vectors for another approach? Most controllers are only too happy to provide maximum assistance if you explain the problem.

Once the crew asked for vectors, the controller had them climb to 4000 feet, since Wurtsmith's radar coverage at Alpena was good only to 3500 feet. The flight dropped from radar again when it descended to 2800 feet outside the marker. The controller turned the flight on the localizer five miles from Felps, but wasn't able to watch it cross the marker due to coverage.

After confirming they had intercepted the localizer, the controller terminated service and approved a frequency change. That was the last anyone heard from the crew until the crash.

With sketchy information available, NTSB could only conjecture as to what happened to the flight. The most likely two explanations were: The intercept heading given by ATC was too shallow and the flight didn't intercept the glideslope until inside the marker, or the flight was blown through the localizer and didn't re-intercept until inside the marker. The latter situation was possible since the winds that night were computed to be:

- 4000 feet - 147° at 18 knots.
- 3000 feet - 126° at 22 knots.
- 2000 feet - 105° at 21 knots.
- 1000 feet - 145° at 12 knots.

The crew could have drifted west of the localizer due to the right cross-to quartering tailwind. This could explain why the crash occurred to the left of the localizer, but this also is pure speculation.

Breakdown in Discipline?

Working on the assumption that the crew didn't intercept the glideslope until inside the marker, NTSB believed the crew flew through the glideslope and became so intent on seeing the lights that neither pilot adequately monitored glideslope indications, altitude or distance.

Another possibility examined was a glideslope malfunction. The FAA flight checked the ILS and found it within normal limits. The two nav receivers were damaged in the crash, leaving investigators unable to determine whether the units worked properly during the approach.

Expectations vs. Reality

Assuming that all equipment operated normally, this accident makes a statement about decision-making and the need for good cockpit discipline. The difference between a true pilot and just another airplane driver is the ability to compare the information you get via radio with what you see out the window and to make a decision that assures a safe outcome for the flight, regardless of where you land.

It's easy to get tunnel vision as you near your destination and the weather is reported close to minimums. In this situation, you might say to yourself, The numbers on the chart say I can do it so surely I'll see something. Whenever a pilot starts an approach with the expectation of making it, without planning for a missed approach and alternate, inappropriate actions almost always result in busting minimums or failing to maintain cockpit discipline.

Dealing With Workload

Flying an approach IMC to minimums is workload intensive. Memorize the missed approach procedure and know where you'll go long before starting the approach. If you're a single-pilot operation, abandon the approach and climb to a safe place if you get lost or confused. This is especially true if ATC radar isn't available. Never be afraid to divert to better weather and go someplace where there's a higher margin for error.

In a two-pilot operation, one pilot should be dedicated to flying the airplane and scanning the gauges at all times while the other person looks for the runway environment. The pilot not flying should monitor airspeed, altitude, positional awareness, glideslope (when appropriate) and should call out any non- standard deviations. The trick is to never break this discipline, no matter how tight the circumstances.

Unfamiliar Approaches

Most approaches flown these days are ILSes. They're used so much that for many pilots the various other approaches are really not much more than procedures to practice during recurrency training.

This is a double-edged sword. Precision approaches are safer, because they provide better guidance to the runway. But flying nothing but ILSes means that we tend to get rusty when it comes to the odd stuff.

We tend to accept whatever the controller hands us for an approach. But if you're not too current, you might want to ask for something a little more familiar and easier to fly. ATC will be glad to accommodate you if they can.

Stick to What You Know

ATC radar has eliminated many tasks for instrument pilots, such as position reports, procedure turns and holding near a busy terminal. The elimination of these tasks allows you more time for cockpit management and position awareness.

The DME arc, like holding, is a seldom-used but nice-to-know procedure. This accident illustrates what can happen when a pilot agrees to fly an unfamiliar procedure. Although the DME arc portion of the approach wasn't the primary cause of the accident, it seemed to have a significant impact on the outcome.

Flew Regularly

The pilot was 66 years old, had accumulated more than 3300 hours and had flown the same airplane regularly for three years. His logbook didn't have any entries for the year preceding the accident, nor was there any documentation showing IFR training or currency.

Available records indicated that the pilot had an initial checkout when he first bought his Cessna 210 and had 21 more hours of instruction during the next month. During the next seven months, he took 60 hours of instrument instruction, then didn't take any IFR training or practice for eight months. He got serious in the next five months and logged 41 hours of instrument instruction, but got a pink slip on his instrument flight test.

He got five more hours of instrument instruction and passed the checkride. Although he didn't keep an accurate pilot logbook after that time, the aircraft logbook showed 285 hours in the preceding year.

Special VFR Departure

The pilot departed Twin Falls, Idaho at 2:30 p.m. for Pasco, Washington (two and a half hours away). He departed on a special VFR clearance, then called Salt Lake Center and air-filed an IFR flight plan to Pasco. Along the way, controllers noted that the airplane wandered about the airways and that the pilot seemed to have difficulty identifying navigational fixes.

Eight minutes after takeoff, the pilot told Center that one of the radios had failed, but he didn't specify whether it was a comm or a nav unit. The accident investigation turned up work orders for radio installation and repair, indicating that all the avionics had been replaced several months earlier.

Low IFR

It was dark when he arrived in the Pasco area. The weather was 400 feet, sky obscured, visibility one and a half miles in fog. The temperature and dew point were both 41°, with calm winds. Although the C-210 had flown through potential icing conditions, nothing indicated that structural icing contributed to the accident.

The primary approach at Pasco was the ILS RWY 21R, a typical procedure except the final approach segment was shorter than usual (3.5 miles instead of the usual 5 miles). The missed approach procedure required a straight-ahead initial climb to thread the needle among several towers and obstructions off the end of the runway.

Cleared for the Arc

Radar was available, but for some reason, the controllers cleared the Cessna to the ILS via the 14-mile DME arc. Approaching from the southeast at 5000 feet, the pilot should have flown inbound to the VOR until intercepting the arc, which he should have flown at 3000 feet.

Apparently, this is where things fell apart, so the situation requires closer attention. We said earlier that DME arc approaches are seldom-used and most pilots aren't familiar with them.

Years ago, we attempted to satisfy our curiosity by reviewing our Jepp manuals to see if there was a pattern or rationale for using these procedures. Our only conclusion was that certain sections of the country had more of them. We don't know if this was due to the approach designer's preference, coincidence or some other reason.

Using a DME arc seems to be a waste of time for light aircraft. Radar vectors can take you directly to the localizer and closer to the glideslope. On the Pasco procedure, you turn onto the localizer 10 miles from the marker, a long segment.

It's a different situation when flying a fast airplane. At 200 knots or greater, the long intermediate segment is inconsequential. It allows a fast airplane to decelerate and get configured for the approach.

There's another benefit for faster airplanes. At 200 knots, a constant 5-degree bank will maintain the arc, doing away with the constant roll-in/roll-out routine required at slower airspeeds.

Initial Turn Okay

The Cessna 210 pilot accepted the clearance via the arc and turned initially in the right direction. The radar track showed that the airplane flew through the arc and began a corrective maneuver, which turned into a three-sixty, the first of several.

There are three techniques for flying a DME arc. We mentioned the first one, which is to maintain a constant bank angle. But that's a tricky maneuver and only works best at high speed.

The second method is to fly a series of short, straight segments and to make heading changes of five or ten degrees to maintain the required distance. To accomplish this, you must figure out ahead of time which way to turn as you go. The radar track indicates this may have been a problem for the Cessna pilot.

With a wind, you may have to hold heading for a bit longer or turn more than 5-10 degrees at a time to stay on the arc. Just like the airways, protected airspace on the arc is four miles on either side.

Ten-Degree Increments

The third method is to intercept the arc and turn the OBS 10° ahead. If you're arcing clockwise, the numbers increase and decrease if you're arcing counterclockwise. Your no-wind heading will always be 90° left or right (as appropriate) of the course selected on the OBS.

For example, if you're flying the Pasco 14 DME arc counterclockwise with the OBS set to 270°, your no-wind magnetic heading should be 360°. When the CDI centers, turn the OBS to 260° and turn the airplane to 350°. By using this method of orientation, the station is always 90 degrees to your left. When you intercept the final approach course of 205°, you must turn 90 degrees left to intercept.

This same method can be used on an HSI with great convenience, since the no-wind heading will always be at the top of the heading card when you turn the OBS to the new value.

Finally, a pilot with an RMI has the easiest arc-flying of all. Turn onto the arc and the RMI pointer will be off the left or right wingtip. When it moves rearward ten degrees, turn the airplane to move the pointer ten degree ahead of the wingtip. Continue this until intercepting the final approach and fly it to the airport.

Must Be Well Practiced

Does this sound like more technique than most pilots have time to develop, especially when the procedure is seldom used, if at all? The FAA Instrument Flying Handbook states, *It is recognized that the pilot, particularly in a single-pilot operation, is too busy during an instrument approach to use formulas for the computation of leads for arc and radial interception, therefore, none are given [in this handbook].*

Unless you are highly proficient in the use of the airborne equipment and in performing arc procedures, it is recommended that DME arcs be flown in IFR weather conditions only when RMI equipment is available.

Pilot Difficulties

The C-210 pilot was obviously having great difficulty with the arc approach, which may have been due to a complete lack of training and familiarity with the procedure, or it may have been the result of avionics problems.

Just before his first three-sixty, the pilot told the controller he was having a problem on the DME arc because one of his radios had failed 15 minutes earlier. A short time later, the pilot said his DME was not working since it was on the failed radio. Shortly thereafter, he reported DME information again. Something wasn't right.

Let's stop for a moment and put ourselves in the pilot's place. If you were in the middle of a DME-arc approach and your DME was intermittent, would you elect to trust it? We wouldn't. If the radio isn't working perfectly, it may as well not be working at all.

All the pilot had to do was ask for vectors...he wound up getting them anyway.

Radar Assistance

The pilot flew two 360-degree turns and a 270-degree turn before getting radar vectors to the localizer. He appeared to track the localizer okay. The Cessna disappeared from radar due to terrain and reappeared when the pilot reported a missed approach. He asked for a clearance to Pendleton, Oregon and crashed moments later.

All components of the airplane were accounted for in the wreckage. The wings and engine were separated from the fuselage, but control continuity was established from the cockpit to the empennage control surfaces. The prop blades had separated from the hub and exhibited twisting, bending and scoring, which indicated that the engine was under power at impact.

The flaps were up and the landing gear was in the process of retraction when it crashed. There was no evidence of preimpact malfunction or failure in the airplane structure, powerplant or any other system.

Constantly Confused?

Based on the available information, it appears the pilot finally got stabilized on the approach, yet he crashed anyway. Why, we'll never really know. Once again, however, put yourself in the pilot's place. You've been struggling with balky avionics. It's dark. You've just messed around flying a screwed-up, looping path all over the sky before the controller finally gave you vectors to the localizer, and, to make it that much worse, you've just had to miss the approach and it looks like you're not going to get to where you want to go tonight. Frustrating? Distracting? You bet.

Confusion reigned throughout the flight: From the special VFR departure (instead of filing from the start), through equipment problems en route, to a lack of knowledge of DME arc procedures and probably, spatial disorientation.

The golden rule this situation is, when in doubt, do something else. If there's no other way to get on the ground except by flying an unfamiliar approach, fly to another airport.

The Circling Approach

T his accident concerns one of the nastiest, most dangerous instrument approaches of all: The circling maneuver at night.

Flying circling approaches is tough enough in the daytime. Throw in the very real risk of disorientation caused by flying such an approach at night and you've got the potential for disaster.

We discussed circling approaches in detail in the last book. Here we'll take a look at how easily a circling maneuver can go wrong.

Running Around in Circles

We encounter some risk every time we move an airplane from the chocks. That risk continues at varying levels until securing the airplane at the end of the flight. The operative word is move, since we are at risk whenever we're in motion. If that motion ceases abruptly or is slowed very rapidly, the results are usually unhappy.

Each step up the aviation ladder increases that risk, e.g., moving from a two-seat trainer to a high performance single introduces more opportunities to get into trouble. The same is usually true when transitioning to a light twin.

Those of us who fly IFR on a regular basis agree that a large amount of risk is removed when operating in the clouds in accordance with a strict set of rules and procedures, where the threat of a midair collision is all but absent.

Naturally, we must be careful about flying into the ground before seeing it, since premature contact with terra firma ranks second only to turbulence-related upsets in the annals of instrument pilots who execute unscheduled arrivals. There are numerous factors which contribute to putting the airplane on the ground prematurely, e.g., low ceiling and visibility, wind shear, navigational errors...the list goes on and on. A combination of circumstances and a build-up of events usually reach the point where the pilot can't handle it.

In the following accident, you can add to that list of factors a relatively inexperienced pilot flying by himself at night in a big, complex airplane to an airport with a non-precision approach.

Air Ambulance Flight

An Aero Commander 681 (turboprop) departed Reno, Nevada at 9:32 pm on a January evening on a FAR 135 air ambulance flight to Winnemucca, Nevada. The pilot obtained a weather briefing an hour and a half prior to takeoff and an update thirty minutes before departure.

The Winnemucca terminal forecast called for a ceiling of 6000 broken, visibility more than six miles, winds from 170° at 15 with gusts to 30 knots until 9:00 pm, with a chance of light rain. The original briefing and the update indicated that the weather was holding essentially as forecast. The pilot filed an IFR flight plan with an estimated time en route of 45 minutes.

Three people were on board the Turbo Commander when it departed Reno and headed northeast; the pilot, a nurse and an emergency medical technician. Their mission was to pick up someone injured in an auto accident. Communications records from Reno Departure Control and Salt Lake Center show that the flight proceeded normally into the Winnemucca area.

The Winnemucca Airport lies at 4303 feet msl and is six miles southwest of the city, almost a way station on Interstate 80 between Reno and Salt Lake City. Like many remote western towns, Winnemucca depends heavily on its airport for quick access to the larger cities, and as a result, the facilities are considerable; the main instrument runway is 6000 feet with medium intensity lighting and a VASI, communications with Reno FSS and a National Weather Service office.

The 30-year old pilot held a commercial certificate with an instrument rating issued two years earlier. His multi-engine rating was almost nine months old. All of his Turbo Commander time (20 hours dual and 40 hours PIC) was in the preceding 90 days. His total time was not determined.

Six weeks before this flight, he flew with his employer (a check airman for his own operation) and was found competent to act as PIC of the Turbo Commander under FAR 135. His authorization included single-pilot privileges using the autopilot in lieu of a second-in-command. (There was considerable post-accident concern as to whether the autopilot was in working order when the airplane departed Reno. As you'll see, it probably didn't make any difference.)

Somewhere along the way, the pilot asked the Salt Lake Center controller to look up the latest Winnemucca weather and was informed that the 10:00 pm observation was not in the system. Even though that observation was never provided to the pilot, it would not have caused concern; with an estimated ceiling of 4500 overcast, visibility 30 miles in light rain, temperature 37, dew point 33, wind 270° at 10, altimeter 29.70.

Cleared for the Approach

At 10:06 pm, the Turbo Commander was cleared for the NDB approach. The pilot requested ATC's assistance in determining his position relative to the beacon, and at 10:15 pm, reported procedure turn inbound. Radar contact was lost three minutes later and the pilot was instructed to change to the advisory frequency.

The FBO at the Winnemucca airport is one of those down home operations in which you'll most likely find the owner/operator on duty early in the morning until late at night. When the pilot checked in and requested the current conditions, the operator (a veteran Nevada airman) advised him that there was a snow shower in progress. The pilot inquired about the ambulance that was to deliver the injured party to the airport, then reported the runway lights in sight.

Apparently, the snow shower prevented the pilot from seeing the runway in time to land on the first pass. One of his unicom reports placed him on a left downwind leg and his last report was turning onto final. By the time the airport operator got the information about the ambulance and tried to call the pilot, there was no response from the airplane.

When it became apparent that a crash had occurred, airport personnel searched unsuccessfully for the airplane. Unknown to anyone at the time, it was on the ground a mile and a half northwest of the airport, totally demolished.

The medical technician on board was seriously injured in the crash. When he was assured that the pilot was dead and that the nurse was badly hurt but alive, he walked to Interstate 80 and flagged down a passing trucker, who called the sheriff's office on his CB radio.

Wreckage Pattern

An on-site investigation was conducted the next day and disclosed that the Turbo Commander came to rest at an elevation of 4250 feet msl, 53 feet below the airport elevation. The first ground strike was 25 feet from I-80 and 30 feet below a small ridge which runs parallel to the highway. The airplane traveled 200 yards up the 20-degree slope on a magnetic heading of 215 degrees. All parts of the airplane were located along this path. It was obvious that the left wing had struck the ground first.

The engines were sent to the manufacturer, where they were completely torn down and judged to have been capable of normal operation at impact. All control cables and major airplane systems were scrutinized and given a clean bill of health. There was no evidence of any physical disability which would have affected the pilot's operation of the airplane.

Why did this Turbo Commander wind up as pieces of junk scattered across a Nevada field? The real answer will never be known, but the evidence certainly points to an instrument-flying procedure fraught with hazard: a night circling approach.

The wreckage was distributed along a 215-degree path and that the pilot's last report was turning final. A turning airplane will continue along a straight path when that turn is interrupted by the ground. With the left wing down in a turn to final, it's easy to determine what happened when the pilot let the airplane get too low.

What happened is clear. Why it happened is not so easy to determine. The airplane was in satisfactory working condition, the pilot was at least minimally qualified, the weather was not that bad and the runway was well lighted. We know that the pilot sighted the runway at some point during the approach—he said so on unicom—but it's likely that he flew into a snow shower as he turned final.

The medical technician (sole survivor of the accident) said that he remembered the landing lights coming on just before the crash and that he couldn't see anything but snow outside the airplane. Disorienting? You bet.

There are no lights between Interstate 80 and the runway. There's nothing but sagebrush and open field, nothing to give a pilot clues as to his height above terrain...a black hole. The airplane struck the ground in a left bank, cartwheeled a short distance up the 20-degree slope and came to rest 53 feet below the airport elevation. Runway 14 was equipped with a two-light VASI, but it was probably rendered useless by the snow shower.

Circling Hazards

A strange airport, unlighted terrain, a sloping approach to the runway, precipitation and an urge to get on the ground all combine to make a night circling approach an operation that demands careful scrutiny and planning if it's to be accomplished safely. It's so hazardous that many corporate flight departments prohibit it's use. If a night circling approach is of that much concern to the pros, those of us who don't fly frequently and regularly should back off and take a second look at the situation.

There's nothing in the rule book which specifies the conditions in which a circling approach may be conducted. In the case of an uncontrolled airport, you're on your own. As long as you observe the circling MDA, and don't descend below that altitude until it's time to land, you've met the regulatory requirements.

There is no vertical guidance of any kind for the final leg of the approach, surely the most critical part of the operation. If there is a VASI available, by all means use it. If there is a visual descent point (VDP) on the chart, put it to work. Light sources (street lights, house lights, shopping centers, etc.) under the final approach path are of inestimable help in this situation. You might be surprised to discover how much you depend on ground lights, especially in an unfamiliar setting.

There's one basic flight precaution which should take precedence over everything else which might have saved two lives at Winnemucca that night. It's so loaded with common sense that we tend to forget about it. When conducting an approach at night—any kind of approach—don't permit the airplane to descend lower than 50 feet above the runway elevation until you see concrete under the wheels.

Fifty-three feet (the altitude shortfall in this case) is not much on the altimeter dial, but a resolve to maintain field elevation plus 50 feet until crossing the threshold is just about guaranteed to keep you from coming to grief short of the runway.

Although it wasn't a factor in this accident, remember that the usual reason for a circling approach is the wind. It usually requires a steeper than normal bank in the turn from base to final. More bank means less lift, which results in a high rate of descent at the normal power setting, and you can find yourself close to the ground in short order.

Whenever things don't look right and don't feel right, they probably aren't. Especially during a night circling approach, heed the advice of your senses and go around. You can always come back for another shot at the runway, with the knowledge of what to expect.

Sad Ending

What a shame that two young people lost their lives and another suffered serious injuries in this accident. In a much less important sense, what a shame that a beautiful airplane was rolled into a ball, never to fly again. As a final irony, what a shame that it was for naught, since the ambulance patient died. If the pilot had been informed of the patient's death only minutes earlier, he probably would have executed a missed approach and returned to Reno.

This was not an accident waiting to happen. It was the result of a series of perceptions, attitudes and procedures which combined to lure the pilot into the black hole short of the runway.

Beware the night circling approach. It is one of the most flexible IFR operations in the book, but it is replete with hazard...and the price of that flexibility is often unacceptable.

Judgment: Pushing the Limits

Managing Risks

In this last section of the book we come to the heart of the matter: Pilot judgment. When we fly IFR, we're presented with a long series of choices to make. Making the right ones means we get to our destination. Making the wrong ones might mean an accident.

As we've already seen, there are many accidents which may well have happened anyway, despite the pilot's poor choices. But these are outnumbered by the accidents that could have been averted had the pilot chosen a different course of action.

Often judgment comes down to a question of limits. How far can you go and still be safe? Are you too tired? Are you current? Is your equipment up to the task?

For this chapter, we'll take a step back and not talk about a specific accident: Instead, we'll discuss the element of risk in flying, and how some pilots ignore it.

Pilots Who Push It

Jimmy Doolittle's blind flying experiments in the 1920s set the stage for those of us who fly in the soup today. There were no rules then and the instrumentation he used was as experimental as the procedures he was trying to prove. But Jimmy Doolittle was a test pilot. His job was to take chances. Our job is to get those who have entrusted themselves to us to their destination safely without taking chances. You read accident reports and wonder why a pilot did something that clearly wasn't safe. Surely the pilot must have known better, but isn't around to explain why. Many accidents involve those who, in the aftermath, are described as safe, competent pilots. Did their luck run out? Did they make a mistake that cost them their lives or did they fall victim to the need to get to their destination no matter what the weather?

Were these pilots pushing it? Did they keep going in the face of problems or were they influenced by external or internal pressures when they should have thought seriously about what they were doing and perhaps sought retreat? Pushing it usually involves bending or breaking the rules, whether it's an FAR or someone's personal minimums.

Busting Minimums

Probably the most frequent violation is busting minimums. It's easy to let the airplane nose down another 50 feet and when searching for the runway environment, even though you're aware that whoever designed the approach restricted it to the published minimums for good reason; obstructions, terrain, missed approach clearances or the MDA or DH is as low as that type of approach will allow.

A King Air was approaching an airport in the Detroit area that didn't report weather. The surrounding area was low IFR with low visibility. The VOR approach, a poor one because it is 25 miles from the station, takes the aircraft directly over the airport at 715 feet agl. The aircraft crashed two miles short of the airport on the approach course, killing the three people on board. The airplane was well below the MDA for that approach.

Was the pilot pushing it, trying to get to his home airport at all costs? Did he set his altimeter incorrectly? Was there a mechanical malfunction? We'll never know for sure, but one thing is certain. The King Air pilot allowed his aircraft to descend below the established safe altitude for the procedure he was using. It killed him and his passengers.

We've often heard pilots talk about how low they can go on a specific approach. The majority of them have their minds tuned to DH or MDA while the others know before they get into an airplane they will push the limits if they need to.

We used to fly with a Citation captain who would allow the airplane to drop 50 feet below the MDA on a non-precision approach. When we called the deviation out to him, he would pick the nose up slightly and regain the altitude before starting the whole thing over. Each time we would call the deviation and each time he would climb back to the MDA. We can't remember one time when that extra 50 feet made the difference between us getting in or not.

Sometimes pilots establish their own minimums for certain approaches. They know they're operating outside established parameters for safe flight, but they do it anyway. For example, one commuter airline, in an effort to increase its trip completion rate into a particular airport, authorized certain captains to fly a localizer approach to 200 feet agl instead of the 659-foot MDA certified by the FAA.

Apparently, the company felt its schedule was more important than safe operation. But why did the pilots put up with it? They knew it was wrong. Was the job that important? Too many pilots get caught in a tug of war between what the FARs require and what their companies demand, sometimes in subtle ways.

At another airport, someone developed a visual VOR approach to a small VFR-only airport. After an accident that killed all aboard a corporate Turbo-Commander trying to get into that field in low IFR conditions, investigators suspected the pilots were using that home-made approach to help them find the airport. They intentionally descended below the minimum sector altitude the controller cleared them to. Again, pilots knowingly disregarded the FARs, and it killed them and the people who had entrusted their lives to them.

In some corporate flight departments without strong leadership or the solid backing of the company's top executives, pilots may feel intimidated into doing things they normally wouldn't. Seldom does anyone say anything, but pilots who disappoint an executive too many times due to canceling a flight for mechanical or weather related reasons might feel their job is on the line if they do it again.

A pilot died in the crash of his Aztec when he busted minimums on a VOR approach because his boss, who died also, pushed him to get to their destination. The pilot, who didn't want to lose his job, threw his professionalism out the window when he descended below MDA in zero-zero conditions.

Several years later, we met the businessman's partner and brother. He told us that pilots were a bunch of prima-donnas who wanted to get paid a lot of money for doing very little. He said someday he'd like to get another airplane, but would fly it himself. We shook our head, but didn't say anything since the man was the customer of our passenger.

Pushing the Equipment

Pushing it isn't restricted to approach and landing, even though it's more likely that accidents will occur when operating near the ground. There was a Cessna 182 pilot that departed an airport in Maine into low IFR conditions. When the pilot got to the airport that day, the battery was dead, so he got someone to jump-start it using cables hooked to an automobile battery.

He took off and shortly afterward lost his entire electrical system. With no radios or navaids somehow he located Boston Logan Airport and attempted to land there. The airplane was destroyed in the ensuing crash landing, but fortunately there were no serious injuries. The pilot had left the master switch on, which drained the battery and there wasn't enough residual power to excite the alternator. From the time he started his engine he never had any electrical power to speak of. He failed to notice the radios were weak or not working properly as he taxied out. Had he turned on the landing light during runup he would have instantly seen a problem in the electrical system.

The pilot probably did what any of us would have done to get his airplane started, but he didn't check the electrical system before launching into instrument conditions. The FARs are clear about the pilot's responsibility to ensure an airplane is airworthy. That airplane wasn't that day and the pilot should have suspected there could be a problem after finding the dead battery.

Some pilots push it and don't realize it. One of the boldest cases we can remember involved an executive of a company we worked for. His company owned an Aztec and he and some of his colleagues flew from southern Indiana to North Dakota. The next day with a heavy snowstorm in progress the Aztec pilot decided to fly home even though the aircraft had no de-icing equipment.

He told the passengers they could go with him or stay. All declined except for the executive. After a crosswind takeoff on a runway covered by heavy snowfall there were several bouts with icing, but somehow the pair made it home while the rest of the passengers waited out the storm and returned on a commercial flight. We often wonder if the others had decided to go that day if the outcome of the flight would have been different. The additional weight in the aircraft might have affected the icing encounters.

There were other stories passed around about this particular pilot. Perhaps it's human nature for a pilot to push the limits just to see just how far he or she can get. But airplanes can be unforgiving and the rules were established with that in mind. Margins were built in to ensure safe operation. When a pilot pushes it those margins disappear quickly, and the slightest error in someone's already poor judgment can kill.

What motivates pilots who constantly push it, risking themselves and those who trust them? It could be an ego problem, or simply the desire to please those around him. It could also be get-home-itis.

Operating on instruments is hard enough, especially for a single pilot. When anxiety levels become elevated because someone is pushing beyond the established limitations anything is liable to happen.

Poor Fuel Planning

The FARs prescribe how much fuel must be aboard at the beginning of an IFR flight. It's your responsibility to maintain the proper reserve fuel.

If you encounter headwinds stronger than expected, it could mean an extra fuel stop. But figuring endurance to the last minute and continuing on because you don't want to make your passengers or yourself late for a meeting is pushing it. What if the weather deteriorates and you wind up with no place to go because you don't have any fuel left over?

Several years ago we were crewing a Citation on a regular run between Manchester, NH and Pontiac, MI. We usually filled all the seats and when the weather was IFR, we couldn't make it non-stop if there was a substantial headwind. The reason was ATCs insistence that we start descending out of FL390 about halfway to our destination. Many times we stopped in Buffalo because it was clear we wouldn't have the required reserve fuel at destination. We could have made it, although we wouldn't have been legal, but it didn't make sense to jeopardize everyone on board for the sake of a fuel stop.

Pushing it is risky business in aviation. A pilot with a professional attitude, regardless of experience and ratings, always makes good decisions that result in a safe outcome. On the other hand, a pilot who gets away with something often gets bolder and pushes it more often. Mr. Murphy has a habit of finding these pilots.

Fighting Fatigue

I*t's an all-too-familiar scenario: Our business is done, and it's time to go home and get some sleep before work tomorrow. Failing to get there means a big hassle: Your boss will be angry at you for not being at work, your kids will miss seeing you again, and your friend Charlie has the airplane signed out for the next morning.*

We must all balance reality (the weather, our condition, and so forth) against expectations (the need to get home) when we fly IFR. What happens when that judgment is made incorrectly is often tragic, as we'll see in the accidents presented here.

Time to Hang it Up

There are days when enough bad things happen during a flight that you should realize it's time to land and wait until tomorrow to tackle the elements again. Sitting in the safety and comfort of a motel room (albeit no place like home) sure beats trying to make it home...at any cost.

If the pilot in this accident had only come to this realization, he might still be alive today. The instrument-rated private pilot was flying his Piper Apache from Bowling Green, KY to his home base in Fall River, MA (a 750-mile trip).

According to his logbook, the pilot had more than 2800 hours (1900 in the Apache) and had flown 22 hours in the last 30 days. Current and skillful were how people described the pilot's ability and the professional manner in which he flew.

The weather for his trip home wasn't going to be smooth sailing. His route paralleled a cold front that trailed from a deep low pressure area in central New York State. During his preflight briefing, the pilot got reports of continuous moderate to severe turbulence along the front at all altitudes due to a strong westerly flow. Icing was also forecast.

Apache N4959P departed Bowling Green on an IFR flight plan at 12:16 p.m. and the flight proceeded uneventfully for several hours at 11,000 feet until over central Pennsylvania. At 3:42, the following conversation took place with New York Center:

Center: Apache Five-Nine-Pop, how is your ride?
N59P: I'd say moderate to heavy turbulence, but I manage to (unintelligible).
Center: Five-Nine-Pop, understand moderate to heavy turbulence.
N59P: Moderate to heavy turbulence, just coming up off the seats every now and then.
Center: Okay, you want lower, sir?
N59P: It seems like it's clearing up now a little bit ahead of me so I'll (unintelligible).
Center: Okay, Five-Nine-Pop, be advised Mode C is indicating you 400 feet above your assigned altitude, so check your altimeter 2960.

The controller cleared the pilot direct Lake Henry Vortac and handed him off to the next sector of New York Center. Contact was established with the next controller, then:

Center: November-Four-Nine-Five-Nine-Papa, New York Center, the Allentown altimeter 2956. Be advised Mode C shows you 300 feet above assigned and let me know when you're ready to copy your new routing.
N59P: Okay, roger, we'll give you a call back for the copy.

This must have been a tiring part of the flight; getting bounced off the seats and fighting to maintain altitude. The pilot showed good presence of mind by telling ATC to stand by until he was ready to copy the new routing. He must have had a handful. Twenty seconds later, the pilot called back and copied the new clearance.

Forecast Accurate

At 4 p.m., another part of the forecast came true:

N59P: Could I get a lower altitude here, maybe down to 9000? I'm picking up some rime ice and it's starting to build pretty good.

After a brief standby, N59P was cleared to 9000 and the controller asked:

Center: November-Five-Nine-Papa, you said that was light rime icing?
N59P: No, I'd say it's moderate. I picked up about a half-inch in about five minutes, so I would say it's probably moderate.
Center: Thank you.
N59P: New York Center, I would like to continue on down through 7000. I am picking up quite a bit of ice.

The pilot was forced to standby once more while the controller coordinated a lower altitude with Wilkes Barre Approach. Forty seconds later, N59P was cleared to 7000. The pilot acknowledged and reported he was still picking up heavy icing. Moments later:

N59P: New York Center, Five-Niner-Papa is still picking up ice and I think I better start looking for an airport.
Center: November-Five-Niner-Papa, roger, let me know what you need. I can get you down to 5000 if you think it will take you out of the icing.
N59P: Well, I might as well proceed down to 5000 and see what happens and then start looking for an airport.
Center: Hazelton Airport would be about your 12 o'clock position and about 25 miles. You would be going into Wilkes Barre Approach airspace and they control that airport.

Controller Assistance
After the pilot acknowledged, the controller got on the line with Wilkes Barre and Harrisburg controllers to find a safe haven for N59P. Less than a minute later:

Center: Piper Five-Nine-Papa, there is a choice. Harrisburg Approach says they've got some small airports to either your three o'clock or your nine o'clock fairly close. If you want, I could switch you over to Harrisburg Approach and they could advise you or if you like I can hand you off to Wilkes Barre Approach.
N59P: Okay, Five-Niner-Pop. I'd like to stay at 5000 and probably go to Wilkes Barre Approach Control. The ice is beginning to melt off now.

He Pressed On
You'd think after fighting turbulence and ice during the four hours of the flight thus far, the pilot would land and take a break for a least a little while. But, having dodged the second bullet, he continued home.

It was dark at 5:12, when N59P was talking to Ocean Approach Control and was told to expect the NDB Runway 24 (the only approach) at Fall River. Since weather isn't reported at Fall River, the pilot tuned the ATIS for New Bedford, MA (8 nm southeast), where the weather was: 300 obscured, 2 miles in light rain and fog, temperature/dew point 56/55, wind 220 at 16. The ceiling was definitely below minimums. The pilot never discussed alternate plans with the controller in the event of a missed approach.

At 5:26, approach called:

Approach: Apache Five-Niner-Papa, eight west of the Fall River NDB, maintain 2000 to the radio beacon, cleared NDB approach, report procedure turn inbound.

The pilot acknowledged.

After crossing the NDB, the radar track shows the pilot flew outbound about two minutes and thirty seconds before starting the procedure turn. He then flew about one minute and ten seconds and turned inbound. With a tailwind during the outbound segment, N59P was getting close to the 10 nm limit for the procedure turn, which prompted a call from approach:

Approach: November-Five-Niner-Pop, are you ready to start your turn back southwest bound?
N59P: That's affirm, I'm just going to get out of this wind up here. I'm just starting my turn now.

The pilot reported procedure turn inbound moments later. At this point, the radar track shows N59P almost seven miles from the airport with a Mode C readout of 700 feet. This prompted a low altitude alert from the controller, which the pilot acknowledged.

At 5:43, the pilot reported the airport in sight and canceled his IFR. Then, one minute later:

N59P: O-Ocean Approach, Four-Niner-Five-Niner-Papa lost the airport.

The controller called back immediately with missed approach instructions, but the pilot never responded. N59P crashed in a wooded area one and a half miles northeast of the airport.

Few Clues Available

The Apache's cabin was destroyed by fire, leaving all instruments and switches unreadable. Investigators were able to rule out flight control and engine malfunctions. Barring a mechanical problem, investigators reviewed the possibility that the pilot got disoriented and lost control of the airplane while maneuvering over the airport. The sequence of events moments before the crash supports this possibility.

During the investigation, the controller who handled the Apache reported: "At 2243 UTC [1743], N4959P reported the airport in sight and canceled IFR. The aircraft went over the airport and made a left [emphasis added] turn northeast bound. About one minute later, N4959P advised he lost the airport. I advised him to climb to 2000 feet over the FLR radio beacon with no response from the pilot. He continued in a turn toward the airport. I called twice more with no response." The last projected position on radar showed the Apache at 400 feet and northeast of the airport.

The controller stated that N59P made a left turn over the airport before the pilot reported losing sight of the field. Since the published missed approach calls for a right turn, this suggests that the pilot might have maneuvered for a left downwind to Runway 24 and lost sight of the runway while trying to fly an abbreviated traffic pattern. This possibility is supported by the radar return, showing the airplane northeast of the field at 400 feet.

Approach Flown

Two FAA inspectors flew the NDB approach at night according to the same profile flown by the Apache. In their report, both inspectors concurred that the approach when flown during a period of darkness, especially single-pilot, would be at best very difficult and disorienting. The approach path, as well as almost every quadrant around the airport, is over a city dump or a water shed area with absolutely no lights on the surface.

Their report also commented on the airport lighting: *There is a low-power Visual Approach Slope Indicator for the instrument runway, but its value is of minor use during a circle maneuver such as that experienced by N4959P. Even the runway lights are of a low intensity design which too is of little value.*

Temptation Abounds

This pilot dodged two bullets (turbulence and ice) during the flight, only to get shot down by a third. The third bullet in this case was fatigue, coupled with a night non-precision approach to a poorly lighted airport. This was the last straw for this pilot after being airborne five hours and twenty minutes. There's something that happens to a pilot's psyche when he/she gets near his/her planned destination, especially when it's home. The temptation to get into a high-risk situation abounds.

After such a grueling flight, the least this pilot could have done for himself was to shoot an ILS at either New Bedford or Providence, neither of which were far away. He flew over Providence to transition for the NDB at Fali River. At best, the pilot could have landed after his icing encounter and waited for more favorable conditions or at least to rest for awhile.

Delayed Search

There's another unhappy ending to this story. The Apache pilot canceled his flight plan after reporting the airport in sight during the approach. While maneuvering over the airport, he told ATC he had lost the airport. The controller issued missed approach instructions, which the pilot didn't acknowledge nor did he answer two subsequent calls from ATC. Watching the Apache's radar and altitude returns close to the airport, the controller assumed the pilot saw the runway and landed.

Four hours later, a man phoned the Ocean Approach Control facility and explained he was looking for an overdue aircraft...N4959P. The controller who had handled the Apache said the pilot canceled his IFR flight plan and had not heard anything further from the flight. Out of concern, another controller called the police and asked them to conduct a ramp check at the Fall River Airport. When the check failed to locate the Apache, search and rescue procedures were initiated, almost five hours after the crash. The wreckage was found the next morning by a U.S. Coast Guard helicopter.

Don't Cancel Early

When shooting an approach to an uncontrolled airport, it's tempting to cancel your IFR flight plan as soon as you have the airport in sight for two reasons: to avoid having to cancel by phone after landing and to avoid holding up other traffic waiting to shoot the approach. This accident points out why you shouldn't rush to cancel. The pilot should have allowed for the possibility of a missed approach. Since he canceled and was out of the system, it didn't occur to anyone that he was overdue.

This tragic scenario also points out the need to have someone who knows your flight itinerary and will contact the FAA if you don't show up on time. Leave explicit instructions for when and who to call. With the toll-free numbers for flight service, it's easy for almost anyone to make the call for you. This procedure is a good safeguard in the event you fall through a crack in the system. When you're down, time is of the essence for survival.

Remember your first "real" approach? Not the first time you shot one in training, but the first one you were able to log as a new instrument pilot. That first approach is an important one: It puts all your brand-new training to the test.

A prudent pilot will do everything possible to stack the deck so that approach comes off easily. Some pilots, however, aren't like that. We've all met them: They feel that the still-wet ticket in their pocket means they can immediately go out and shoot an approach to minimums on the proverbial dark and stormy night. Legally, they can...and they're likely to make it.

This story is about a brand-new instrument pilot who was not only inexperienced, he'd stacked the deck against himself in other ways. There's little doubt he was tired...he hadn't had much sleep, or much to eat, for that matter.

Running yourself down like that is a certain way to make hash of your judgment abilities, as we'll see here.

The First-Timer

If you ever hear a golfer claim "I'm *never* nervous on the first tee," don't believe anything else he says. Even when the first hole is well down on the handicap list, there's a certain amount of concern about what's going to happen with that first shot. You might have hit a bucket of balls long and straight on the driving range, but every golfer is a little antsy when it's time to keep score.

The difference between the accomplished golfer and the duffer is the knowledge of his capabilities and limitations. When you're reasonably sure where the first shot will go, you can move the ball—steer it around hazards and handle whatever extraordinary circumstances might be present. The inexperienced (or perennially inept) golfer will likely do better in the long run by playing it straight. No trick shots, nothing fancy. Stay in the fairway even if it costs you a couple of strokes.

This philosophy might also be applied to an instrument pilot when cleared for the approach in IMC. Especially when you're new at the game or just plain rusty from lack of practice, there's a lot to be said for doing nothing out of the ordinary; fly the procedure as published with no shortcuts or unusual maneuvers and if you see something you don't like, go around.

This accident involves a pilot who began his instrument training in March and achieved the rating at the end of August in the same year. At that time, his logbook showed a total of 245 hours (almost all of it in his Mooney 201), 36 hours of hood time, 10 hours in IMC and two hours in a simulator.

When he started home on the evening of the accident, his solo IFR experience consisted of 1.3 hours of instrument time on a trip two days before. All of the time was logged en route, with no approaches. The procedure during which the accident occurred was apparently the first time he had flown an approach by himself and also was his first solo night IMC approach.

Setting the Stage

The accident happened near the end of a long weekend; not long in terms of time, but long in terms of the pilot's activities. On Friday evening, he had flown his Mooney from Leesburg, VA (10 miles northwest of Washington-Dulles) to western North Carolina and back, then spent a sleepless night due to family problems. (Notice the chain starting to build already.)

Saturday was taken up with church activities, including the beginning of a two-day fast. The lack of sleep was aggravated by a lack of nourishment and he only got about six hours of sleep on Saturday night. The fast continued until Sunday afternoon, when the pilot planned to repeat the North Carolina trip. He might have stopped at a fast-food restaurant on the way to the airport, but there was no firm evidence in this regard.

Shortly after noon on the day of the accident, the pilot got a preflight briefing from Washington Flight Service. A front was across Virginia from northwest to southeast and was responsible for 800 and 3 conditions in the Leesburg area. The forecast called for steady improvement during the day. The destination, on the west side of the front, was comfortable VFR and forecast to remain that way.

The pilot filed an IFR flight plan and departed Leesburg late that afternoon. Although he flew to North Carolina without incident, the FBO manager there recalled that the first landing attempt was hot and high. The pilot executed a go-around and tried again, the second time touching down half-way on the 4000-foot runway. The pilot also took an inordinate amount of time to run through the engine checks before takeoff. Where the effects of fatigue and hunger beginning to show?

At 9:45 p.m., the pilot was on his way home, once again on an IFR flight plan. He left the Center frequency and called Washington FSS (on the airport at Leesburg) to check weather:

FSS: Dulles is reporting 1000 overcast and three miles in fog, temperature 68, dew point 65, wind south at four knots. We're out here at Leesburg and there's some drizzle and mist falling out here now. Conditions appear to be lower than those reported at Dulles.
Pilot: Is it moving at all?

FSS: Negative, we're not expecting much improvement until, well, they're expecting better conditions after midnight, but it hasn't shown much improvement over the last couple of hours.

There's no evidence the pilot got a briefing before leaving North Carolina. This suspicion was underscored by his first request when returning to the Center frequency: he said he would need an alternate and asked for Dulles Airport to be added to his flight plan.

The remainder of the en route portion of the flight was routine. When the pilot checked in with Dulles Approach at 7000 feet, he was told to expect the VOR approach to Leesburg and was offered a critical piece of advice: There's problems with the runway lights at this time at Leesburg. Several aircraft have missed due to not being able to pick up the airport; the runway lights are too low.

Weather worse than forecast and a problem with the runway lights. Neither would be terribly significant to a pilot with a reasonable amount of IFR experience and enough smarts to realize that Plan B might have to be executed. As it turned out, the pilot-controlled lighting system was inoperative. Someone had stolen the antenna during a taxiway construction project, which meant no matter how many times the mike was keyed, the runway lights wouldn't budge from their medium intensity default setting. No notam had been issued, but the controller's words were real-time information.

Two professional pilots had made approaches into Leesburg earlier that evening. One was able to circle and land, while the other couldn't see the runway lights in time and elected to land at Dulles. In both cases, visual acquisition of the runway or one of its lighting systems made the difference. FAR 91 requires that you make a missed approach if at least one of the required visual references isn't picked up in time to complete a normal approach to the runway surface.

Seventeen minutes later (immediately following hand-off to the approach controller responsible for the approach into Leesburg), the Mooney pilot was again made aware of the runway lighting situation: "Be advised several inbounds into Leesburg tonight reported the lights to be very dim."

The Final Moments

The pilot was vectored to the final approach course and cleared to cross Fuzzi Intersection at or above 1500 feet. He was cleared for the approach four miles from Fuzzi. The controller added the usual reminder to cancel IFR, terminated radar service and cleared the pilot to change to unicom.

The radar plot shows the Mooney tracked the final course reasonably well to the Runway 35 threshold. At that point, there are six rapid clicks on the approach control frequency, clicks that were later analyzed and determined to come from the Mooney. It was the wrong frequency, the wrong number of clicks and much too late to be useful for a straight-in approach.

The pilot rolled into a three-sixty to the left just as he reached the threshold, a maneuver that might have been prompted by a last-minute acquisition of the lights or an attempt to stay at 9.3 DME while searching for the runway. The Mooney rolled out somewhat to the left of centerline, flew the length of the runway and crashed into a field a half-mile west of the departure end.

The impact attitude was 28 degrees nose down, in a left bank of 35 degrees, with the gear and flaps up. The wreckage path (only 115 feet) and apparent low airspeed suggested disorientation and loss of control. The pilot didn't survive.

Lessons Learned

Specialists at Washington FSS were interviewed by NTSB. Several of them had completed their shifts within the hour before the accident and although they didn't make official observations as they went out the door, they recalled the visibility and ceiling were very low at the airport (estimated as low as a half-mile and 400 feet).

One of the pilots who had approached Leesburg that evening remembered he hadn't spotted the runway lights until he was almost over the threshold and they were dim. He was able to keep the lights in sight, execute a low-visibility circling maneuver and land.

The other pilot didn't see the runway lights at all and noticed the airport beacon out the side window as he started a missed approach.

There was also pertinent information from the pilots of a helicopter operating in the immediate vicinity of the airport. These pilots decided to land due to low visibility and helicopters aren't subject to measured visibility minimums. Several other witnesses mentioned thick fog, rain and low clouds around the airport. It seemed that the weather at Leesburg was indeed worse than what was reported at Dulles.

The information about the pilot's activities and behavior before and during his very first solo IFR trip was developed after the fact. The pilot must have known his own physical and mental condition. Should he have attempted the trip, even if it wasn't this first IFR shakedown cruise?

There are no regulations with specific prohibitions against such a flight. Once you have an instrument rating and use it under FAR 91, you're on your own. Controllers don't ask how you feel before issuing an instrument clearance and passengers depend on you for the most objective assessment of your capabilities to deliver them safely to the destination.

Effects of fatigue

The Airman's Information Manual has some good advice about fatigue and its affect on pilot performance:

Fatigue continues to be one of the most treacherous hazards to flight safety, as it may not be apparent to a pilot until serious errors are made. Fatigue is best described as either acute (short-term) or chronic (long-term).

A normal occurrence of everyday living, acute fatigue is the tiredness felt after long periods of physical and mental strain, including strenuous muscular effort, immobility, heavy mental workload, strong emotional pressure, monotony and lack of sleep. Consequently, coordination and alertness, so vital to safe pilot performance, can be reduced. Acute fatigue is prevented by adequate rest and sleep, as well as regular exercise and proper nutrition.

Chronic fatigue occurs when there is not enough time for full recovery between episodes of acute fatigue. Performance continues to fall, and judgment becomes impaired so that unwarranted risks may be taken. Recovery from chronic fatigue requires a prolonged period of rest.

Degrees of Stress

Stress comes in for its share of discussion in the AIM as well:

Stress from the pressures of everyday living can impair pilot performance, often in very subtle ways. Difficulties, particularly at work, can occupy thought processes enough to markedly decrease alertness. Distraction can so interfere with judgment that unwarranted risks are taken, such as flying into deteriorating weather conditions to keep on schedule. Stress and fatigue can be an extremely hazardous combination.

Most pilots do not leave stress on the ground. Therefore, when more than usual difficulties are being experienced, a pilot should consider delaying flight until these difficulties are satisfactorily resolved.

Emotion is also discussed:

Certain upsetting events, including a serious argument, death of a family member, separation or divorce, loss of job and financial catastrophe, can render a pilot unable to fly an aircraft safely. The emotions of anger, depression and anxiety from such events not only decrease alertness but also may lead to taking risks that border on self-destruction. Any pilot who experiences an emotionally upsetting event should not fly until satisfactorily recovered from it.

Whether a multi-thousand hour pilot or one with a brand-new certificate or rating, we aviators all have something in common: the psychological and physiological effects of fatigue are insidious, self-perpetuating and hazardous. A fatigued pilot can easily develop perceptions of urgency that override good judgment. Get-home-itis is a real disease, with results that are all too often terminal.

Safe Haven Available

This accident could have been easily prevented. The pilot had a solid-gold alternate (Dulles Airport, only 10 miles away), with decent weather and several ILS approaches. Although there was nothing illegal about his decision to attempt the approach to Leesburg, he should have had his antennae up when informed of the probable lower-than-forecast weather and problems with the runway lights. At the first sign of anything out of the ordinary (no visual contact with the runway lights a mile out), he should have been cocked for a missed approach. When the missed approach point was reached with obviously no hope of making a normal descent and landing, there should have been no question—power up and get out of there right now.

A Smart Pilot Knows

A smart golfer swings a bit easier on the first tee, knowing it will probably improve the quality of that important first shot. A smart instrument pilot carefully considers the consequences of an approach under less-than-ideal conditions, especially when he's new at the game and hasn't flown on the gauges for a long time. He who approaches and flies away will live to approach another day.

This story is similar to the last in that the pilot worked a full day before the flight and failed to eat, yet he still felt it necessary to go rather than stop for some rest.

An added dimension is that several people, including his father, recognized that he was trying too hard to get home and urged him to postpone the flight. Had he listened, the worst that would have happened was the loss of a vacation day from his job.

Listen to Your Elders

One benefit of teaching student pilots to fly standardized traffic patterns is that they soon learn to make changes to accommodate whatever wind is blowing. Either the pattern or the power must be adjusted to get the airplane to the runway. It's a matter of energy management.

This principle also applies when you're flying into the teeth of a wind during a cross country flight. In this situation, you must add power to compensate for the headwind or accept a lower groundspeed. The latter is usually better, since a high power setting can drastically reduce your range. Again, it's energy management.

It's also important to manage your personal energy, especially during a long flight. In this accident, the pilot strung himself out to the point where he probably couldn't make good decisions. He was determined to reach a far-away destination by morning.

Long Day's Journey

A flight from Lakeland, Florida to Lubbock, Texas is a long haul in a Cessna 172. Under no-wind conditions, it takes nine hours for this flight of more than 1100 miles. With a westerly wind and an average groundspeed of 90 knots, the flight time increases to 12 hours, a full days work for any pilot.

There were two pilots in the C-172. The owner had 925 hours total time and the other pilot had 130 hours. This arrangement could have worked with one pilot flying while the other slept and by taking frequent fuel/rest stops. They departed Lakeland after dinner, so the entire flight was in the darkness of a winter night.

The pilot in command (the owner) got up at four o'clock that morning and worked a normal day. He skipped breakfast and ate a big meal at lunch. He had planned to take an afternoon nap, but never did. To complicate matters further, he didn't eat dinner.

Good Advice Ignored

The two pilots departed Lakeland at 7:30 p.m. for Panama City (250 miles northwest). They arrived in Panama City three hours later and had the airplane refueled.

The pilot called his father (who lived in Texas), since they had originally planned to stop and visit along the way. Time became more important than fatigue. He told his father they were bucking headwinds and couldn't stop, so they would fly directly to Lubbock. The pilot said he didn't want to use any more vacation from his job.

The father recognized the problems created by the long day and urged the pilot to stay overnight in Panama City. Employees of the FBO also tried to talk the pilots into taking a rest, but to no avail.

By midnight, they were two hours out of Panama City and the pilot had been up and running for 20 hours. They contacted the McComb

(Mississippi) Flight Service Station and asked for the winds aloft. We don't have a record of the numbers that were provided, but they were indeed bucking headwinds, with a groundspeed of less than 90 knots.

Weather Devils Watching

One hour later, the New Orleans FSS got a call from the pilots, asking for the current conditions at Alexandria, Louisiana. Unfortunately, the Alexandria FSS had closed for the night. The nearest weather observation was at England Air Force Base (18 miles away), which was 600 overcast with a partial obscuration due to fog and calm winds. The discussion with flight service continued.

Pilot: New Orleans, we have...in other words, ah, Alexandria is ah...is it below minimums for an ILS approach there now...on your...RVR factors?
FSS: I have no reports for Alexandria. I say again, I have no reports from Alexandria. The England Air Force Base weather is now clear, visibility three miles in fog.
Pilot: All right sir, thank you. We'll go over there and see what it looks like. Thank you, sir.

The pilot in command still didn't file an IFR flight plan or ask for radar service. He was a CFII, and had signed instrument training in the other pilot's logbook, but had not logged any actual instrument time in the past six months. He may not have considered himself current and was reluctant to file.

The Vise Tightens

More than four hours had passed and the pilot must have been concerned with the dwindling fuel supply, to say nothing of his dwindling personal endurance. There's an interesting comment in the NTSB report that reveals how the effects of fatigue were setting in:

Reviewing a copy of the tape of this communication [with the New Orleans FSS] revealed no problems with the aircraft's radios. Rather, the pilot's rapid speech and jargon were difficult to understand. There is some doubt that the pilot comprehended the weather situation depicted by New Orleans Radio.

There was no further communication from the C-172. At 2:45 a.m., two people that lived less than 300 yards from the accident site heard a single-engine airplane flying very low over their houses before it crashed. They lived beneath the final approach to Runway 26 at

Alexandria Airport and were familiar with the sound of aircraft landing there.

They reported that the engine sounded normal and the aircraft was quite low. The sound of the engine was continuous to impact with the trees.

Both of their spouses were awakened by the crash, and one (a highway patrolman), reported the accident and started a search. Although the aircraft was less than 150 yards from his house, he didn't locate the wreckage until 5:30 a.m. because of the fog. The pilots didn't survive.

Few Good Answers

Why was such a long flight attempted after a long day? Fatigue creeps up like a thief in the night and steals judgment in liberal amounts. Perhaps the derogation of good decision making is the most hazardous loss of all.

Once in a bad situation, even when sorely fatigued, most of us experience a surge of energy and alertness. But even the most heroic physical effort can't overcome a bad decision. Accident investigators surmised that the pilot descended below decision height two miles short of the runway.

Why didn't the pilot get an IFR clearance when it was apparent that he would need an instrument approach to land? This accident should be of value if for no other reason than to point out the benefits of asking for an instrument clearance when needed, whether you're current or not.

Radio Problems?

The investigation reviewed the possibility of a radio problem, since the aircraft's transponder was set to 7600, the radio failure code. Unfortunately, the answer could not be determined. Houston Center's tracking program was down for maintenance, so no transponder was detected and no flight path information was available.

Why did the pilot attempt an approach at Alexandria when there was better weather at other airports in the area? The most reasonable answer seemed to be a grave concern about the fuel supply. If this was the case, the time to make a decision to land and refuel should have been much earlier, when they could have landed VFR. Fatigue probably robbed the pilot of good judgment.

Get-Home-Itis Prevails

Faced with all the negative aspects of this flight, why did the pilot launch in the first place? Our perception of our personal capabilities is nurtured by a disease that is pervasive and overwhelming. It's known as get-home-itis, and it infects all of us at one time or another. How successfully a pilot staves off an attack often determines whether he lives to fly another day.

Be aware and be alert. Get-home-itis (the art of pressing on) and airplane accidents are closely related. It's much better to be safely on the ground, wishing you were in the air, than to be in the air and in trouble, wishing you were on the ground. There's always another day.

Watching
Your Fuel

H ere's something you can hang your hat on: People operate motorboats, automobiles, motorcycles and other powered vehicles right up to the last drop of fuel. If that weren't true, the spare gas can manufacturers would get into some other line of business.

Pilots aren't immune from this problem. The crash of Avianca 052 proved that this isn't the sole province of amateurs.

Many general aviation fuel-exhaustion incidents/accidents result from an "I think there's enough fuel on board" attitude, plus the pilot's determination to get to the destination. Even when the gauges show that the end must be near, some fliers press on, overflying airports, hoping that the powerplant will keep churning until the destination is reached.

The regulations absolutely demand that you never leave the ground under IFR unless there's enough fuel on board to reach your destination, fly to an alternate (if required) and still have 45 minutes of fuel on board.

There are rather stringent requirements that, if followed religiously, eliminate any concern about running out of gas. Weather briefings play a large part in this area of flight operations, since there are times when aircraft range and weather conditions are incompatible. Sometimes, you simply can't go, if you follow the rules.

In the accident that follows, weather conditions and "gotta get there" played leading roles, with a large supporting cast of other considerations.

The Fine Art of Corner Painting

It's 645 nm from Long Island, NY to Atlanta, GA, a long trip in a single-engine airplane.

The fact that it was flown late at night by one pilot makes it even longer.

The National Transportation Safety Board (NTSB) report doesn't contain much detailed weather information, but we know that the pilot got a telephone briefing from the Islip, New York Flight Service Station. Given the low-IFR conditions at the end of the flight, we can assume that the pilot was aware of other than CAVU conditions along the route and at his destination.

The Cessna 210 lifted off Farmingdale, NY at 11:50 p.m. and the pilot got his IFR clearance to Peachtree-Dekalb Airport almost immediately. Within five minutes, the flight was level at 6000 feet and continued southwest without problems, and almost no radio communications. If you've ever flown in the wee hours you know that life gets boring and complacency hangs heavy.

Four hours and 15 minutes later, the C-210 approached the Atlanta area at 6000 feet and talked to Atlanta Center:

N92S: Atlanta Center, this is Nine-Two-Sierra.
Center: Nine-Two-Sierra, go ahead.
N92S: Nine-Two-Sierra, I'm running a little low on gas. I'd like to stop in Athens [30 miles east of Peachtree-Dekalb and was only a few miles closer at the time. A little low on gas may have been the understatement of the day—Ed.]
Center: Cessna Nine-Two-Sierra, cleared to Athens via direct, maintain 6000.
N92S: Nine-Two-Sierra, roger.
Center: Nine-Two-Sierra, descend and maintain 3000. The airport is at twelve o'clock and about eight miles. Let me check the weather real quick.
Center: (20 seconds later) And November-Nine-Two-Sierra, the weather at Athens is indefinite ceiling one hundred, sky obscured, one-half mile visibility in fog and the altimeter is 29.91. The wind's one-eighty at six.
N92S: (After a few seconds of digesting the unhappy information) This is Nine-Two-Sierra, does anybody else around here look any better?
Center: Let me check Peachtree real quick. That's gonna be the closest one with any weather reporting, sir.
N92S: Roger.

The Center controller called Atlanta Approach and asked for a recent observation for Peachtree-Dekalb. "Son, I ain't got the slightest idea. They don't tell us a thing at night," replied the approach controller.

Peachtree weather observers had gone home several hours before and it was now 4:15 a.m.

The weather at Atlanta-Hartsfield Airport was much better: 900 broken, 3500 overcast, three miles in light rain and fog. This information was given to the pilot.

Center: November-Nine-Two-Sierra, Hartsfield's got 3000 broken.
N92S: This is Nine-Two-Sierra, Peachtree is my destination, but I was hoping to stop before I got there. I may hang on for a little while longer.
Center: Okay, I don't have any weather reporting available at Peachtree right now and Athens sounds pretty bad. Hartsfield's the only place close that's got any decent weather that we know of.
N92S: Nine-Two-Sierra, roger.
Center: Do you want to go on to Atlanta Approach and then decide which airport you want to try and land at?
N92S: Yes sir, I think I'll do that.
Center: Roger, how much fuel have you got, sir?
N92S: Well, if I can trust my gauges, I've got about 45 minutes worth and I should be about 20 minutes from Atlanta.
Center: According to our computer, it's gonna take you 26 minutes to get to Hartsfield. You're doing 140 knots.
N92S: Roger, how long would it take me to get to Peachtree?
Center: About the same time. Maybe a minute or so less, but like I said, we don't know what the weather is like there.
N92S: Roger, any chance of getting the weather by telephone?
Center: Approach Control's been working on it, but I don't believe there's anybody at the airport to take an observation at this time of night.
N92S: Roger, Nine-Two-Sierra.

A considerable amount of coordination was taking place behind the scenes as N92S continued emptying its fuel tanks. The C-210 was close to the localizer for the ILS at Peachtree-Dekalb and was handed off to Atlanta Approach Control. The plan was to vector the C-210 for an ILS to Peachtree, and if that didn't work out, the controller was all set to take the airplane straight to Hartsfield.

Just before handing off N92S to Atlanta Approach, the Center controller mentioned, "He's getting kinda panicky." The 45-minute fuel supply had been over-estimated and the pilot had painted himself into a corner.

Atlanta Approach picked up the C-210 when it was 31 miles east of the airport and told him to fly 270° to intercept the localizer. The pilot said he was indicating 140 knots. Four and a half minutes later, he was only nine miles closer to the outer marker. The corner was getting smaller.

Approach: Nine-Two-Sierra, you must have a pretty strong wind. It appears as though you're tracking northwestbound. Turn left heading 250.
N92S: Nine-Two-Sierra, left 250 and feel free to cut me in close to the marker. As close as you can.
Approach: Yes sir, we're trying to get you right there at the marker, but there is a pretty strong wind and it appears as though you're going pretty slow. It's hard to tell as for the trail of your target and it appears as though you're tracking northwestbound.
N92S: Roger.
N92S: (One minute later) Nine-Two-Sierra, I think I just ran out.

Nothing Left

Nothing more was heard from N92S. The C210 came to rest in a vacant lot and both occupants died. Investigators found two teaspoons of gas in the fuel system, which led them to the pilot's operating handbook and a calculation of the probable fuel-burn profile for the flight:

Taxi and takeoff .... 2.0 gallons
Climb .... Cruise (4.6 hrs @ 18 gph) 82.8 gallons
Total fuel burn .... 87.1 gallons
Total usable fuel .... 89.0 gallons

Even if the investigators' calculations were way-off, this pilot cut deeply into whatever reserve he might have had.

Other Factors

The cause of this accident appeared as straightforward as they come, e.g., the pilot flew until all the fuel was gone. But there's more to this accident than simple fuel exhaustion and a lot to be learned by instrument pilots.

First, fatigue, one of the most insidious thieves of pilot awareness and decision-making, was a factor. The NTSB report doesn't go into detail on this point, but it seems reasonable that the pilot worked a normal day before taking off at midnight. There was no evidence of sloppy flying or gross inattention during the flight, but the pilot's mind may have worked in strange ways when deciding to press on. Time of day was probably also a factor. Most of us aren't nocturnal creatures and when we undertake mind-intensive tasks in the wee hours when we're supposed to be sleeping, our usual good judgment may be warped.

Second, a perceived need to complete the trip (get-there-itis). There was plenty of evidence that this pilot intended to get to Atlanta, no matter what. The two men were expected at a business meeting in Atlanta at 10 a.m. They held airline tickets for the trip, which were found in the wreckage. Unfortunately, they were bumped from the flight, and since they had to get there, decided to fly themselves.

Third, they should have divided this long trip into smaller segments, if for no other reason than to refuel so they could approach their weathered-in destination with plenty of time in the tanks to accommodate delays or diversions. No one likes to interrupt a smooth flight with a refueling stop, but it's much more comfortable when you know there's extra gas to work with.

Knowledge of the airplane you're flying is another very important factor in a situation like this. This pilot had logged 69 hours in Cessna 210s, owned N92S and had flown it four hours in the last 90 days before the accident.

It's also interesting that three cylinders had recently been replaced and the engine was operated at 75 percent power to seat the rings. While this is a normal procedure, the investigation also revealed that the pilot adjusted the EGT 200 degrees cooler than peak during the break-in period. This is very conservative, and good for new cylinders, but that knowledge should have been a major part in the pilot's planning for this trip.

Be Conservative

The accuracy of aircraft fuel gauges has been questioned many times. Some indicators are very good, while some are accurate only within certain ranges, while others aren't accurate at all. It's important to know what you're looking at and the only way is to make periodic checks on gauge accuracy. Develop a worst-case fuel scenario for your airplane, using the most conservative figures and arrive at a time-in-the-air limit that you will never violate. Make this time at least one hour short of your conservative dry-tanks estimate.

Make it a habit to estimate the gallons required each time you top off. This little game will force you to check gauge accuracy on a continuing basis and will make a faulty gauge or change in fuel burn stick out like a sore thumb. Be even more conservative and suspicious of fuel consumption with rented or borrowed airplanes, especially if you don't operate a particular airplane on a regular basis.

Respect the instrument flight rules that pertain to fuel requirements. These rules are in the books to force you to do what common sense tells you is right. When there are no alternates within legal fuel range of your airplane, do something else.

If there's ever a time when the gremlins will strike, it will be in the dark when all the airports within your reach have gone below minimums. Running out of gas on a clear day with plenty of forced-landing options below is one thing; running out of gas on instruments at night is something else.

Finally, are you aware of the most fuel-efficient configuration for your airplane? Do you know what power setting has the best chance of getting you safely home in a fuel-poor situation when you really need to squeeze out every mile? This pilot apparently pressed on at normal cruise power to the end, when a significant power reduction may have gotten him to Peachtree with the engine still running.

Aviation, like the sea, is not inherently dangerous, but it is terribly unforgiving. The world of flying is filled with corners. Take that extra measure of precaution so you don't paint yourself into one.

Many pilots have experienced either a low-fuel situation or at least the unsettling feeling that there might not be enough petrol on board to complete the mission. Those who go through the low-fuel grinder usually do so only once and vow never again to find themselves aloft with less than one hour's fuel in the tanks. The mental strain, the concern for the passengers' welfare and the potential embarrassment simply aren't worth the risk.

The Incredible Luck of the Irish

One of the best ways to defeat the fuel-exhaustion monster is to be knowledgeable about your aircraft's fuel system; how much it burns, the accuracy of the gauges and how power settings can enhance the range. In this story, all that knowledge and experience was present, but ultimately ignored. The commercial pilot had 434 hours in the Cessna 402, all of it by himself in an operation that required relatively long flights. As you'll see, he had the fuel consumption rates and gauge indications calculated to a fine point. Nevertheless, the fuel monster bit him. Here's how it happened.

He Walked Away

The sun lightened the Kentucky countryside long before it rose that

October morning, due to the clear skies that prevailed all night. As might be expected that time of year, heavy fog developed, and when the half-light penetrated the mist, a Cessna 402 could be seen on the ground at Madisonville Airport. It sat lower on the ground than normal, since the landing gear had been sheared off in a powerless crash-landing the night before.

The Cessna was 150 feet from and perpendicular to the runway. All was quiet, because the pilot (a beneficiary of the good fortune that benefits those with Irish surnames) walked away from the crash.

The flight began as a routine night cargo run from Jackson, Mississippi to Detroit, Michigan with stops at Tupelo, Mississippi and Evansville, Indiana. The pilot was briefed in person at the Jackson FSS before the flight and fog was forecast for nearly all Kentucky airports.

The pilot flew VFR from Jackson to Tupelo, picked up additional cargo, and was soon airborne again. Aware of the possibility of instrument conditions at Evansville, he air-filed an IFR flight plan, obtained a clearance and proceeded northbound.

At 0125Z, just beyond Paris, Tennessee, the pilot asked Evansville Approach Control about their current weather and was advised, "Well, we're an eighth of a mile in fog. A DC-9 missed the approach just a couple of minutes ago. We don't expect any improvement in this fog situation until about 10 o'clock in the morning."

The pilot acknowledged and said he would continue and see how things looked as he got closer.

Three minutes later, another pilot on the frequency reported that visibility at Owensboro Airport (25 miles southeast of Evansville) was zero-zero. This probably prompted another inquiry from the Cessna 402 pilot, to which the controller replied, "Evansville is still one-eighth of a mile. Nobody's landing."

Within the next four minutes, radio conversations indicated that the fog was getting thicker, with visibility dropping to one-sixteenth of a mile. The Cessna continued.

FAR 135 Rules

This flight was a commercial operation subject to the rules of FAR Part 135. One section of that regulation states:

No pilot may begin an instrument approach procedure to an airport unless the latest weather report indicates that weather conditions are at or above the authorized IFR landing minimums for that airport.

There's considerable question about the legality of the flight to Evansville in the first place, since FAR 135 operators cannot file IFR to an airport unless the forecast indicates that the field will be at or above minimums upon arrival.

The pilot probably saw the lights of Paducah, Kentucky as he flew northbound and pressed on. He flew two ILS approaches at Evansville and, as you might imagine, both of them ended in missed approaches. Both used what by now became precious fuel.

Diversion

Following the second missed approach, the pilot asked for radar vectors to Henderson Airport, where there was an unofficial report that the visibility was one mile. This was another violation of FAR 135, since all weather reports for commercial operators must come from official sources.

He reported the beacon in sight and was cleared for a contact approach. When a unicom conversation revealed that there wouldn't be any fuel available until morning, he broke off the approach and told Evansville Approach that he needed to go somewhere else. (More fuel wasted.)

At this point, there was probably one hour of fuel in the tanks. The pilot appeared to be more concerned about refueling and continuing with his cargo to Detroit than getting the airplane on the ground. (How we can be led astray by our perceptions of priorities).

Concerned about his fuel state, the pilot asked to leave the frequency to get weather information. The pilot found that Bowling Green, Kentucky (about 80 miles southeast of Evansville) was reporting VFR conditions. He asked for and got an IFR clearance to Bowling Green.

The two missed approaches at Evansville and the flight to Henderson greatly affected fuel quantity. Additional vectoring was necessary while the pilot obtained weather from flight service. When he was finally cleared to Bowling Green, the pilot said he had 40 minutes of fuel remaining. From his position over the Evansville VOR at 0235Z, he calculated that he would run out of fuel at 0315Z (keep that in mind).

Tempted to Divert?

The pilot made a good decision, based on his knowledge of the time remaining. At 0252Z, he was handed off to Memphis Center for the remainder of the flight, but two minutes later, something was wrong.

At 0254Z, the pilot asked for an immediate vector "...to an airport with a beacon." This turned out to be Greenville, an airport for which he didn't have an approach chart. The controller provided the numbers for the VOR approach. The pilot reported shortly thereafter that the airport was in sight and that he would try a contact approach.

The Cessna disappeared from radar and radio contact for seven minutes, when a very concerned pilot came back on the air and reported a missed approach. He was climbing to 3000 feet and flying to the Central City VOR.

The controller asked about his fuel status and the pilot replied, "...estimating about twenty minutes." He elected to try the full VOR approach and said, "Please let me know when I'm over the airport."

The pilot's confidence in his fuel gauges may have slipped, or he was unwilling to believe his fuel calculations, or perhaps he was tempted by the rotating beacons of a couple of small airports along the way.

If the pilot's estimate of 40 minutes remaining from Evansville was correct, the airplane could have flown well beyond Bowling Green and have plenty of fuel for an approach and safe landing. Once again, keep in mind that all-important 40 minutes and the fuel-exhaustion time of 0315Z.

At 0309:33Z, radar showed the Cessna overhead Greenville, but the pilot couldn't find it in the fog. He circled in vain, and at 0309:58Z, the controller (having received a report from another pilot) advised that the Sturgis Airport was wide open. The controller provided a heading for Sturgis and told the Cessna pilot that the distance was 15 or 20 miles at the most.

Luck Runs Out

Control of the airplane was transferred back to Evansville. At 0312Z, the pilot reported five minutes of fuel in the right tanks and 15 minutes in the left. He was close, but not quite on the money. One minute later, he was back on the air with the unhappy news that the right engine had just quit and declared an emergency.

If that weren't enough, the controller informed him that the earlier estimate of the distance to Sturgis was wrong and he had 40 miles to go. With not much choice left, the pilot said, "Okay, I think we should be able to make it in there."

Within seconds, the pilot reduced his fuel estimate to five minutes, and followed closely with, "Okay, wouldn't you know it...we got some trouble, can't get the right one feathered here." The reservoir of Irish luck was rapidly running dry.

It was now 0315Z, the time of fuel exhaustion based on 40 minutes remaining when the Cessna departed Evansville. If the flight had continued to Bowling Green as planned, the airplane would probably be safely on the ground. Instead, at 0315Z, when advised that Sturgis was still 30 miles away, the pilot said, "I'm not going to make that. Got about 10 minutes of fuel on board."

The controller advised that the Madisonville Airport was a few miles straight ahead. Although heavy fog was reported there, this was the proverbial port in the storm, so the pilot asked for a vector.

Three miles out, The pilot sighted the airport beacon, but the leprechauns weren't quite ready to smile on this Irishman. The beacon was visible, but ground fog obscured enough of the surface to make a normal approach and landing impossible.

At 0323Z, the pilot reported, "Okay, we're heading in at 900 feet. We're heavily loaded and we need to find that airport and make one shot at it." A minute later, with great resignation, he said, "It quit. We're going in."

The airplane crashed in a plowed field on the airport and slid to within 150 feet of Runway 05/23. The accident report states that, "The pilot exited the aircraft and walked to the airport office for assistance."

Situation Influences Decisions

This pilot surely sweated bullets as one option after another closed that night. It's a safe bet that he wished he had considered more carefully considered the operational rules, which, if observed, would have averted the entire problem.

Setting that aside, we must commend him for knowing the airplane so well. The right engine quit within two minutes of his calculation. We can only wonder why he didn't continue to Bowling Green. You can probably imagine yourself in his place, hoping that the fuel calculations were correct and agonizing as the airplane seemed to move at a snail's pace through the air.

Our perceptions of circumstances and subsequent decisions are frequently distorted by the situation itself. 'Twould be a cool pilot who could ride through an experience such as this and not be tempted to go for a nearby airport as the fuel gauges moved toward empty. There are times when we must persevere if we want to attain the objective that has been set after careful consideration of the facts.

One final thought. If you happen to be a wearer of the green and count on your traditional good luck to bail you out of a tight situation, don't push it. Remember, the author of Murphy's Law was also an Irishman.

Weather Gambles

W e close this book with a look at what makes instrument flying necessary in the first place: Bad
weather.
As we noted at the beginning of the book, most accidents involving weather
are caused by inadvertent flight into it. When the weather is a factor in an
accident that brings down a qualified IFR pilot, it's usually only one of several
underlying causes.

When it comes to really bad weather, however, it's often the most important
factor in the ultimate outcome. The accidents we present here are all related to
the weather, but always with other factors thrown in.

The Thunderstorm Wins Again

Each of us has reasons for obtaining an instrument rating. Perhaps
your flight training took place in the military, in which case there was
no choice; your reasons and Uncle Sam's were the same. Maybe IFR
capability represented a personal challenge, an opportunity to move to
a higher plateau of achievement, whether or not you intended to put
the rating to use.

The most prevalent reason for civilian pilots adding IFR capability
to their credentials is the flexibility it adds to aviation operations and
the concomitant increased usefulness of an air plane in business. No
more waiting for the visibility to creep above three miles so you can
leave, no more changing plans and canceling trips because the weather
is bad between here and there. With an instrument rating, the general
aviation airplane is a marvelous means of transportation.

The central character in this story is just such a pilot. Successful in a business which required a lot of travel throughout the southeast, he soon figured out that his effectiveness could be enhanced by a personal airplane. He progressed through several lower performance models to a turbocharged Cessna 210 in order to move more rapidly between business locations.

A fast, high-flying airplane is severely limited when its pilot can't fly in weather, and less than two years after receiving his private pilot certificate, this gentleman became an instrument pilot. Unfortunately, he didn't have much of a chance to put his new capability to use. When his aviation career ended, he had 308 hours, 30 hours in the C-210 and 44 hours of instrument time, only four of which were actual IFR (in the presence of his instructor).

Incremental Experience

Experience in the instrument environment is probably more important than experience overall as a pilot, because unusual, unexpected and frightening weather encounters can be very critical to your survival. The way to go about gaining this experience is beautifully documented by Robert N. Buck in his classic book, *Weather Flying*. In the chapter, "Teaching Yourself to Fly Weather," Buck says:

"The idea is to fly weather with safeguards that relate to our experience. After we've flown the first step's conditions enough to feel comfortable, we can take on a little more as in step two, and so on. The steps are:
1. Fly good weather to good weather on top.
2. Bad to good.
3. Good to bad.
4. Bad en route.
5. Thunderstorms."

Captain Buck proceeds to explain in great detail how a beginning IFR pilot should pace himself, taking on the increasing demands of weather flying as his experience grows, sneaking up on the weather. Experience in weather flying is not so much the improvement in your instrument flying skills as it is an understanding of the need to assess what's going on around you in relation to your capabilities and those of your airplane. Of course, with experience comes the ability to make good decisions regarding weather.

The flight we're going to discuss here was the very first time this pilot put his instrument rating to work, the very first time he was out in the IFR world for real by himself. Do you remember your first actual IFR experience? It is quite likely embedded in your memory just as firmly as other major events in your life. Like the pilot of the Mooney earlier in the book, the first was also the last.

Frontal Thunderstorms

Weather conditions in the southeast U.S. during March are often characterized by cold fronts moving smartly from the northwest, creating considerable turbulence in and around the frequent thunderstorms that develop. The nastiness of these weather systems is usually exacerbated by the Great Smoky Mountains, whose northeast-southwest orientation parallels most cold fronts. Such was the case on March 21st, several years ago.

The NTSB report provides a good recap of the weather briefing:

At 5:08 pm, a specialist at the Hickory (North Carolina) Flight Service Station administered a weather briefing to a telephone caller who identified himself as the pilot of N6117R. The briefing was for an IFR flight from the local area to Chattanooga, Tennessee. According to the briefer, the weather was generally VFR all the way at that time, with scattered thunderstorms en route. Terminal forecasts were calling for generally VFR conditions, except IFR conditions in scattered showers or thundershowers.

A sigmet contained in the Washington Area Forecast was given, pertaining to thunderstorms possibly in lines or clusters developing in advance of the cold front. The sigmet also contained a warning of moderate to locally severe turbulence, associated with these thunderstorms. An airmet, also contained in the Washington Area Forecast was given concerning moderate turbulence below twelve thousand feet over the area.

Pilot reports were given stating that at 3:30 pm, 30 miles north of Nashville, the pilot of a Aztec encountered a thunderstorm, heavy rain showers, small hail, light clear icing and moderate turbulence at nine thousand feet. Also, the pilot of a Cessna 401 reported severe turbulence at eight thousand feet between Chattanooga and Crossville, Tennessee.

The current radar report indicated an area of scattered rain showers and thundershowers 30 miles northeast of Chattanooga. The pilot was advised it could be rough if he encountered any thunderstorm activity; he stated that he would ask for radar vectors around the thunderstorms, and would take a southern route to get around the mountains, as he did not want to fly over them.

At the conclusion of the weather briefing, the pilot filed an IFR flight plan for departure from a small airport 20 miles northeast of Charlotte, direct to Charlotte VOR, then V194 to Anderson VOR and V5 to Chattanooga. Even though V194 no longer exists, and the Anderson VOR is now Electric City (ELW), the essence of the route is unchanged. The pilot chose a southern route to stay away from the mountains, but would probably have to penetrate the cold front and the associated convective activity.

At that time, VFR conditions prevailed at both departure and destination, and the situation certainly implies with Buck's advice to start out by flying from good weather to good weather (except that between the good weather points you should be able to fly on top). A springtime cold front producing thunderstorms could hardly be considered "on top."

The C-210 departed around 5:30 pm and shortly thereafter was cleared to Chattanooga as filed, to maintain six thousand feet. The flight was subsequently cleared to eight thousand and approaching the Greenville, South Carolina area, the pilot of N17R requested current Chattanooga weather, which was: 4600 broken, 9500 overcast, visibility ten miles in light rain.

An hour after takeoff, N17R was handed off to Atlanta Center.

Center: One-Seven-Romeo, you're in radar contact.
N17R: Roger, Center, and I'd like to climb to nine thousand please.
Center: Ah, One-Seven-Romeo, unable nine thousand at this time, I'll see if I can get it for you in a few miles.
N17R: That's okay, we'll stay right here. Eight thousand looks pretty good right now.

There's no indication in the record of a good reason for the pilot's request for a higher altitude, but we can assume that he encountered either some lower clouds ahead of the front, or some uncomfortable turbulence due to wind flow over the Smokies. The next significant conversation took place just a few minutes later:

Center: One-Seven-Romeo, I'm showing an area of precip ahead of you. It lies directly across your line of flight and it runs in a line from northeast to southwest.
N17R: Okay, ah, how about vectors around that precip?
Center: Roger, One-Seven-Romeo, turn further left heading 230, that ought to keep you out of the weather I show on radar.
N17R: Roger, heading 230, thank you.

This was not working out as planned. Instead of flying westbound toward the turning point which would take him to Chattanooga, the pilot of N17R found himself headed southwest, getting farther from home by the minute. Then the situation began to compound itself:

Center: One-Seven-Romeo, Atlanta Center, I'm showing a wide area of heavy precipitation directly ahead of you about 50 miles.
N17R: (After a thoughtful pause) Ah, roger, what's the latest Chattanooga weather?
Center: One minute here, let me look it up for you. Okay, the latest observation at Chattanooga was measured 3400 broken, 6500 overcast, visibility nine miles in very light rain showers, surface winds 240 at 13. And there's also a pilot report from a commuter turboprop, reported severe turbulence and downdrafts over the mountains coming into Chattanooga.
N17R: Okay, and I've got quite a bit of lightning off my 2 o'clock position, that's probably the precip you're showing on radar.
Center: Yeah, I think so. If you want, I can take you further south and west, out near the Rome VOR. It looks like that would take you around all the precip that I'm showing.

The route proposed by the controller was an end run around the weather and would put the Cessna almost 50 miles due south of Chattanooga before it could turn northbound. At this point, N17R was slightly southeast of the Nello Intersection and the pilot apparently didn't want to waste any more time flying out of his way.

Critical Communications
Now, two crucial communications took place. In the first one, the pilot of N17R asked "How's it look direct Chattanooga?" And the controller answered, "Looks good direct Chattanooga." The pilot may have been asking about observed weather on the direct route and the controller may have thought the pilot was asking about a clearance direct to Chattanooga. Either way, the answer "Looks good direct Chattanooga" was a loaded gun. The pilot considered his options (go direct to his destination or fly the end run) and made his decision:

N17R: Okay Center, One-Seven-Romeo, I'll go direct Chattanooga and I'd like six thousand please.
Center: Roger, One-Seven-Romeo, you are cleared direct Chattanooga, descend and maintain six thousand. You can deviate north or south as necessary for weather.
N17R: One-Seven-Romeo is cleared direct Chattanooga at six thousand

and I'll need some help around the precip. I can still see lightning up ahead.

Center: Alright sir, the only way I can help you around it would be to take you west about 35 miles. You've got a solid line. (And here comes the second critical communication) However, aircraft have gone through it, and said it's just been light to moderate precip and light turbulence.

N17R: Alright sir, we'll proceed direct Chattanooga, that'll be the easiest way.

Led Astray?

If there was ever a situation in which a controller's comment may have led a pilot down the garden path, that was it. But before you condemn Atlanta Center, keep in mind that the pilot had seen lightning ahead of him on his in tended route of flight. He knew of thunderstorms and severe turbulence from both his preflight briefing and the pilot report he had just received. We should also keep in mind that the controller had absolutely no way of knowing the pilot's IFR experience level. Such knowledge would have been moot anyway, since the pilot in command is the pilot in command.

Minutes later, N17R reported level at 6000 feet and requested further descent to 4500 feet, to get under the clouds. The controller was unable to assign anything lower than 6000 feet at that point, but advised he could comply with the request in another ten miles as the flight was over high terrain about then. We pick up the communications three minutes later:

N17R: Ah, Center, this is One-Seven-Romeo, I've got ah moderate turbulence and a lot of lightning here at 6000. I need to go down to 4500.
Center: Understand, One-Seven-Romeo, I can't get you any lower right now. You've got a four to five mile stretch of heavy precipitation, then you should be in the clear.

No answer from N17R. It's a good bet that the pilot had his hands full; a brand new instrument pilot on his first trip by himself in weather, at night, over the mountains, flying in moderate turbulence and lightning. It was three minutes later when everyone on the frequency came up in their seats:

N17R: Mayday, Mayday! I just about got torn apart! There was severe turbulence...thunderstorms...just about got turned over. I'm at 3500 feet!

That was the last transmission from N17R. Thirty-five hundred feet was not enough altitude. The C-210 impacted a mountain ridge at 2930 feet msl, destroying the airplane and killing the pilot. During the post-accident investigation, photographs taken of the weather radar display at Athens, Georgia showed a heavy build-up in the immediate vicinity of the accident site. N17R had flown into one of the thunderstorms forecast, reported and observed along the route of flight.

Could a more experienced pilot have handled the turbulence which upset N17R? Possibly, but what a terrible chance to take. Even it were possible, that last segment of the flight sounds something less than an enjoyable ride.

Would a more conservative pilot have accepted Center's suggestion for a deviation around the weather, even if it meant flying another 50 miles? Probably, and the additional time would have been a small price to pay for getting home in one piece.

Dependence on ATC Radar

There's another factor which was crucial in the outcome of this flight, something which is still operative today even in the face of a great deal of pilot education. That factor is the dependence of some pilots on ATC radar for guidance through areas of convective activity.

The lawsuit which resulted from this accident generated an in-depth study of what the controllers observed on their screens and what was actually out there that night. It turns out that storms were developing along the front just like waves on the ocean. The Atlanta controller mentioned that there was a solid line and that aircraft penetrating it experienced only light turbulence, but those aircraft apparently passed above the worst of the storms, in the troughs of the waves. When N17R got there, things were entirely different.

One lesson is clear, perhaps more so today than when this accident occurred: pilots must not depend on ATC radar for penetration of thunderstorm areas. Today, all ATC radar is limited to computer-generated images and weather returns show only at two preset levels. The controllers have no way of making qualitative determinations when they see precip returns. The primary reason for ATC radar is traffic separation, not weather avoidance or penetration.

Another lesson for instrument pilots leaps from the record of this accident: When starting out in the IFR business, don't challenge all of the dragons on your first solo flight in weather; side-step into weather encounters ala Robert Buck, so that you'll know more of what you're doing when the chips are down.

Finally, given the destructive potential of even a small thunderstorm, don't allow yourself to get caught inside a cloud in a thunder-storm area unless you have radar or Stormscope on board and know how to use it. Depending on a controller to pull all your chestnuts out of the fire isn't fair to either party.

Commuter airlines often find themselves in a tough spot. Operating on a shoestring to begin with, they have powerful incentives to meet schedules, yet the equipment they use isn't able to deal with bad weather as well as that flown by the major air carriers.

The setup for the accident that follows is not all that uncommon: The weather was good enough to start the flight legally, but began to deteriorate en-route. It was hovering at the ragged edge right up to the last minute. In a situation like that, a commuter pilot is highly motivated to try and complete the flight rather than screw things up for everybody by diverting unnecessarily.

Anything You Can Do, I Can Do

If the guy in front of me makes it, I'll try it, is an aeronautical rule-of-thumb that's been used by pilots of all experience levels through the years. Using it as the sole basis for making decisions can be deadly, especially during the thunderstorm season, as the pilots of a Beech 99 commuter found out a few summers ago.

L' Express Flight 508 departed Mobile, AL on a hot July afternoon with 13 passengers, bound for Birmingham, AL (a one-hour and 10 minute flight). The weather briefing the captain got before departure indicated he would have thunderstorms to deal with at Birmingham; a typical summer afternoon in the Deep South.

The flight was at 9000 feet, navigating Victor 209 southwest of Brookwood Vortac and talking to Atlanta Center. At 5:45 p.m., they tuned in the Birmingham ATIS (almost one hour old), which reported the weather as 5000 scattered, visibility 10 miles, temperature/dew point 92/72 and the wind from 80° at eight. Simultaneous approaches were in use to Runways 23 and 36.

TRW as Forecast

Even though the ATIS didn't mention them, thunderstorms were moving in as forecast. The cockpit voice recorder (CVR) revealed the pilots were evaluating the building weather both visually and on their weather radar. Minutes later, Flight 508 asked Center for a northeast heading around the weather. Deviation right of course approved, when able direct Vulcan [Vortac], replied the controller.

Flight 508 was then cleared down to 6000 feet. The crew started their descent checklist and monitored the new ATIS broadcast:

Birmingham weather, measured ceiling 4200 broken, visibility seven miles, thunderstorms, temperature 84, dew point 68, wind 350 at eight. Large thunderstorm northwest of airport moving southeast, east moving southeast. Thunderstorm began at 40 past the hour. Low-level wind shear advisories in effect. ILS Runway 5 approach is in use, landing and departing Runway 5, Runway 36...

The crew was 46 miles south of Vulcan Vortac. The first officer, either looking out the window or at the weather radar remarked, "Pretty big guy. That's the one that's northwest of the field."

"We should be able to get under that, I mean go around that," remarked the captain.

Running for Cover

While Flight 508 was still on the Center frequency, the thunderstorm they were discussing had pilots in the Birmingham area running for cover. "Attention all aircraft, the field is now IFR and visibility two," announced Birmingham approach.

A Learjet, five miles southwest of McDen LOM, was intercepting the Runway 5 localizer for the approach. Flight 508 came on the frequency just in time to hear the Lear pilot say, "I think we better make a left turn here and go out and hold for a while. It looks pretty bad on radar."

Shortly thereafter, a Piper Navajo inbound to the field announced he was turning away from the storm. The controller gave the Navajo pilot a place to hold and told him the thunderstorm "...is right over the airport moving southeast bound. Looks like it's gonna take probably at least a half hour or 45 minutes before it gets out of your way."

The captain of Flight 508, obviously thinking about their next move, remarked to the first officer, "Well now, what about this?"

While everyone else was contemplating options, a Piper Aerostar (who seemed undaunted by the weather) was inbound on the ILS. Birmingham approach called Flight 508, "Lex Five-Zero-Eight, just to let you know what's goin' on, I had a Lear set up on the base from the southeast for the ILS to 5. He got in a little close and saw something on the radar he didn't like, so he turned off the approach and he's holding right now. I do have an Aerostar on the approach and he's on about a two-mile final right now. We're trying to get a ride report out of him."

Suddenly, everyone's attention focused on the Aerostar. It reminds you of the television commercial where the kids are afraid to try the cereal and say, Let's see if Mikey likes it!

Approach continued vectoring Flight 508 to the localizer. Finally, the controller announced the long-awaited news:

Approach: Lex Five-Zero-Eight, the Aerostar said the ride wasn't all that bad, but the rain had the visibility down to just about zero until they got to three-quarter-mile final. He did pick up the airport, but he said the ride wasn't that bad, if you want to try it.
508: Understand, Five-Zero-Eight, we'll try it.
Approach: Lex Five-Zero-Eight, is 11 miles from McDen. Maintain 2600 until established on the localizer. Cleared ILS Runway 5.

The crew completed their approach briefing, then:

Approach: Lex Five-Oh-Eight, I'm going to hold you on until you get to the marker. That way, if you have to break out for something you don't like, you'll be ready. [This is really getting tight—Ed.]
508: Okay, sounds good. What's your visibility now, Five-Oh- Eight?
Approach: Visibility is two and one-half, thunderstorm and rain showers.

The captain cautioned the first officer to be alert for wind shear and said, "If you don't feel comfortable about this, let me know."

"Okay, so far it's all right," was the first officer's reply.

This was followed by one last exchange with Approach:

Approach: Lex Five-Zero-Eight, how's the ride so far?
508: So far, it's good. A little bit of rain and pretty light.
Approach: Okay, Lex Five-Zero-Eight, contact the tower 119.9. We'll see ya.

The crew never contacted the tower. Seconds later, the CVR recorded the captain calling for climb power, followed by the sound of increased engine speed. Another few moments passed and the captain called for full power. Then, the recording stopped.

The Beech 99 crashed into houses about one mile outside the LOM and burst into flames. Only the captain and one passenger survived.

Thunderstorm Penetrated

The controller who vectored the flight told investigators he saw an area of broken precip about four miles in diameter on his display, which was along the final approach course for Runway 5. The circular polarization for the radar was turned on, which meant only the heaviest precipitation would appear. Flight 508 was last seen on radar at 2300 feet and entering a broken area of precipitation 6.5 miles from the runway.

Things must have gotten pretty hairy after this point, since the evidence indicates the airplane went through a series of violent maneuvers before coming out of the clouds and hitting the ground.

Investigators found Flight 508 had penetrated a thunderstorm of at least Level 3 intensity (on a scale of 1-6). The National Weather Service classifies a Level 3 thunderstorm as strong with heavy precipitation. Apparently, another cell moved in or the same cell grew in intensity after the Aerostar flew the approach.

Dynamic Weather

There's a feeling of deja vu connected to this accident. About 20 years ago, a B-727 was on an approach to New York-Kennedy International with severe thunderstorms in the area. Another airliner had just missed the approach, reporting wild airspeed fluctuations and loss of altitude. Meanwhile, as the crew of the B-727 discussed the wisdom of continuing, a Beech Baron success fully completed the approach. The Baron pilot reported heavy rain and not a bad ride, having made the approach between two areas of severe weather.

The B-727 crew continued their approach based on this report. Unfortunately, another thunderstorm had moved across the final approach course and the airplane crashed short of the runway. This was a landmark accident in that it prompted the research leading to what we know about wind shear today.

Both the B-727 and Flight 508 accidents underscore how rapidly weather changes during the thunderstorm season. A block of airspace that's okay to fly through one minute might be deadly to fly through five minutes later. During the prime thunderstorm months of July and August, convective clouds build rapidly, especially during late afternoon. What appears as a benign build-up can develop into a full-blown thunderstorm in as little as 20 minutes.

Even airborne weather radar can deceive you in this situation, since what appears to be just a lot of rain can become severe in minutes. Some of the newer airborne radars are better at detecting wind shear and turbulence, but these units come with a hefty price tag.

ATC Radar

Also keep in mind the limitations of ATC radar in depicting thunderstorms. Circular polarization is used to filter out all but the most severe precip on a controller's display to reduce interference with aircraft targets. A controller can't watch the weather build until it finally pops up on the display, which means it's already well on its way to being severe.

While you'll probably get general guidance from ATC as to the heaviest returns, there can be hazardous stuff to be avoided that hasn't shown up yet.

Don't Trust Mikey

When other pilots are holding to wait for severe weather to pass, you should expect to do the same or land somewhere else and wait it out. Be wary of anyone who manages to squeak in under these circumstances. Sound the alarm if you ever find yourself saying, Gee, the guy in front of me made it, so I'll give it a try. Instead, say to yourself, "That guy was lucky to make it, I'll wait until I know I can."

Ice is one of the scariest phenomena the pilot of a small airplane can encounter. It can't be seen on radar or any other electronic gadget like a thunderstorm can: The best anyone can do is issue a forecast for conditions favorable to its formation, which is imprecise at best, and provide pilot reports, which are fleeting in their accuracy.

This is the story of a pilot who had an icing encounter and managed to successfully battle the beast all the way to his destination, only to be struck down almost literally at the runway threshold by a weather hazard of a different sort. Notice that the pilot of this airplane was doing the right things: He was updating his weather, and rather than press on he actually made a precautionary landing to wait it out. Unfortunately, he didn't wait long enough, choosing instead to press on.

An Ironic End

The pilot, an attorney and instrument flight instructor with 734 hours, owned a Piper Turbo Lance. Shortly after lunch on December 31, he loaded his family and ski gear into the Lance and departed Wilmington, Delaware for Rutland, Vermont.

Ski Weather

The weather was better for skiing than flying. Most of the trip would be on instruments. The briefing had warned of icing and moderate turbulence with low-level wind shear. These were normal conditions for the last day of December, but the Lance wasn't equipped for flight into known icing.

Lance N2243J departed Wilmington at 1:30 pm, having been cleared as filed for the 250-mile trip. Twenty minutes later, the pilot requested a lower altitude due to ice.

N43J: Allentown Approach, Lance Four-Three-Juliet with you at 6000 and we're in the soup picking up a little bit of frost and would like to know if I can get down to 4000 on this route of flight.
ATC: Lance Two-Two-Four-Three-Juliet, Allentown Approach, altimeter 3021, you can expect an altitude change in seven miles.

This was a very polite pilot, but when you encounter icing in an airplane that isn't equipped for it, there's no need to be nice. If you need a lower altitude, let ATC know, with authority.

There was no response from N43J, and for the next several minutes, the controller tried to reestablish radio contact. Four minutes later, the controller called in the blind and cleared the Lance to 4000 feet. Shortly thereafter, the controller noticed that the airplane had drifted off course, so he gave a vector to rejoin the airway. Finally, N43J called back explaining, "We had a radio problem. We're back with you and proceeding right turn 330 to Victor 149."

Three minutes later, the controller was forced to clear N43J to 5000 feet due to a traffic conflict. The altitude change must not have been a problem, since the pilot had no comment.

Concern Builds
At 2:10 pm (near Wilkes-Barre, Pennsylvania), the pilot asked about the weather.

N43J: Wilkes-Barre, Four-Three-Juliet, have there been any pireps on tops in this area?
ATC: Four-Three-Juliet, no, sir. I don't have any pireps right now.
N43J: Do you know what the forecasted tops are in this area?
ATC: Standby, sir. I'll see what I can find for you. Eight-Four- Sierra, How's your flight conditions at 6000?
N84S: Okay, I was gonna call you. We broke out of the soup just about over Hazleton Vortac. We have a broken deck below that's estimated maybe at 5000 for the tops and we also have a scattered deck above us.
ATC: Okay, sir. You're pretty much between layers now?
N84S: That's affirm. We had very light icing in the clouds.
ATC: Roger. Four-Three-Juliet, I got a guy about 20 miles southwest of

your position. He's in between layers at 6000.

N43J: Okay, Four-Three-Juliet, thanks very much. We'll take an altitude change if you can give it to me. Let's try 6000. (Mr. Nice, again. How about, Approach, 43J requesting 6000. It's short, assertive and easily understood.)

ATC: Okay, Four-Three-Juliet, climb to and maintain 6000. I'm painting some weather right in front of you, but it looks like in another five miles you should be pretty much through it.

N43J climbed to 6000 and broke out between layers within a couple of minutes. The pilot left the frequency to check weather and the following discussion ensued when he checked in with Binghamton Approach.

ATC: Lance Four-Three-Juliet, did you get a hold of Elmira Flight Service, sir?

N43J: Yeah, I got a hold of Elmira all right. According to the weather there, Albany [New York] is reporting indefinite ceiling, sky obscured, three-quarters of a mile in light snow showers and Rutland [his destination] does not report. The weather is obviously gonna turn worse. I really doubt this approach can be made. We're gonna have to consider options on landing short of that. What's your weather in your area right now?

ATC: Lance Four-Three-Juliet, Binghamton weather, we're measured 2300 overcast, visibility 25 and we're making visuals to Runway 16.

N43J: Four-Three-Juliet, tell you what I'll do, that looks good for now, think I'm gonna divert to Binghamton. I'd like a clearance to Binghamton and land at your airport and sit this one out. [Good idea!—Ed.]

ATC: All right, Lance Four-Three-Juliet, fly heading 310, maintain 6000. You're cleared to the Binghamton Airport via radar vectors, left traffic, visual approach Runway 16, maintain 6000.

A Good Move

After landing, the pilot called flight service and got the same information as before. By now there were two pireps of light to moderate icing and turbulence. I'll think about it and call back later to see if there's any improvement, said the pilot.

When he called back 30 minutes later, the situation hadn't changed. In the meantime, however, he had called Rutland and was informed by an unofficial observer that the airport was good VFR, with a ceiling above 3000 feet. The briefer repeated the precautions for icing and turbulence and added several more pireps. The pilot said he wanted to file an IFR flight plan and would be ready to go in 15 minutes. Was good reason being eroded by a desire to hit the ski slopes?

The pilot had seen fit to stop part way to Rutland because of the weather, yet he only waited about an hour before proceeding. That's not much time for the weather to improve sufficiently.

N43J was airborne again at 4 pm. Even though the briefer had made it clear that there weren't any reported tops, the pilot had filed for 9000 feet, probably hoping to get on top. He reported out of the clouds while climbing through 7500 feet, with only a thin layer above at 9000 feet.

The pilot called Burlington FSS to find out about the conditions at Rutland.

N43J: We're en route to Rutland. Any current weather and altimeter setting for Rutland or Poughkeepsie or anything close to it?

FSS: I don't have a Rutland altimeter setting. You'll have to contact them on unicom. I can give you a note on the book there [referring to the approach procedure—Ed]. You're supposed to increase the MDA to 2800 feet.

N43J: Okay, I understand, without Rutland altimeter I'll increase MDA to 2800, thank you. Any weather at Glens Falls [30 miles from Rutland] right now?

FSS: Roger, the current weather at Glens Falls is estimated 1800 broken, 2500 overcast, the visibility is seven miles. Temperature 20 and the wind is 210 at eight, altimeter 3012. You really should check with unicom as far as any altimeter setting.

Getting Down

A commuter flight just off Rutland reported the ceiling at 2500 feet msl, visibility five to seven miles, wind calm. That would be okay for the normal LDA approach with an MDA of 1680, but without the local altimeter, an MDA of 2800 feet made completion of this approach unlikely.

N43J approached Rutland from the south-southwest and was cleared to cross Ira (the IAF) at or above 6000 feet and cleared for the LDA approach. The pilot had to fly the approach without vectors.

Shortly after clearing N43J for the approach, the controller noticed that the Lance would miss Ira by at least three miles. When the controller called N43J about this, the pilot responded, "I show having crossed Ira already. What do you show on yours? Maybe my NDB is not working properly." (Ice on the antenna?)

The controller vectored the Lance back to Ira and on to the localizer. After the first turn, the pilot reported moderate ice. Then, radar contact was lost due to terrain.

ATC: Okay, I've lost you on radar, sir. You're gonna have to resume your own navigation and proceed direct to Ira. If I pick you up on radar as you proceed towards it I'll call it for you, but I've lost you now. You'll have to resume your own navigation.

N43J: Lance Four-Three-Juliet, we're getting some ice now. I'd like to proceed up to try to get out of this right now, okay?

The controller immediately cleared the Lance to 8000 feet, but things were going downhill rapidly.

N43J: We're experiencing a problem up here. We're having a very difficult time climbing up to 8000. Maintaining six. I'd like a course to clearer weather, if necessary, back to Binghamton.

ATC: Two-Two-Four-Three-Juliet, roger. Okay, maintain 7000 and fly heading 290. We'll try to get you in radar contact.

N43J: 290 degrees.

ATC: And your option, six or seven thousand feet if you want to try to climb out. I understand 7000 was clear of the ice.

N43J: Okay, we'll try to get up to seven, thank you.

ATC: Piper Two-Two-Four-Three-Juliet, I'd like to confirm your altitude as 6000 feet. You say you're level at six now?

N43J: We're at 6000 feet, but I'm negative on the climb right now.

ATC: Okay, are you sure your altimeter is reading correct? You may have ice on some of your static systems.

N43J: Yeah, Four-Three-Juliet, I believe that's correct. Appears the pitot heat's on and I think it's reading correct.

N43J was just not climbing at all, according to the pilot. The Lance was finally picked up on radar and given vectors to Burlington, Vermont. The weather was 3500 overcast and 15 miles visibility.

The airplane was so badly iced that it couldn't maintain 6000 feet. The best the pilot could do (with great difficulty) was 5500 feet. The terrain between him and Burlington made vectors around the mountain necessary.

ATC: Two-Two-Four-Three-Juliet, are you still accumulating ice, or is it, has it kinda stopped accumulating?

N43J: Four-Three-Juliet, we're accumulating ice. Our heading now is 350 degrees and we're actually losing altitude with the ice.

The pilot then asked the controller to "get us to Burlington and try to provide radar vectors onto the ILS as quickly as possible." Clearly, time was of the essence.

The pilot asked for a surveillance approach, followed quickly by a request for "the lowest area around here that I can land. I'm trying to maintain 5500, but I just can't do it. I'm gonna have to declare an emergency."

Almost...

When N43J was 18 miles from Burlington and apparent safety, the controller cleared the Lance down to 4500 feet, then to 3500 feet and finally to 2000 feet. The pilot voiced a heartfelt "thank you" with each lower altitude.

ATC: Four-Three-Juliet, the present heading looks good. We'll put you on a right downwind for Runway 19, that's most aligned with the winds right now. They're about 170 to 180 at 20 to 30 knots.
N43J: That'll be just fine. (At a time like this, who cares about strong winds?)
ATC: And Four-Three-Juliet, are you losing some of the ice or do you still have a lot of it on the aircraft?
N43J: It's definitely coming off. I do have a lot of ice covering the windshield. I can see out, visibility's about two to three miles with the windshield problem.
ATC: Okay, I'll vector you right on to final, Four-Three-Juliet.
N43J: That would be great, thank you.

The pilot must have thought he just about had it made. The airplane was shedding ice, and he was nearing a safe haven. Unfortunately, the light at the end of the tunnel was to prove to be an oncoming train.

When the Lance was five miles out, the tower controller could see the airplane's lights. It was dark, but the pilot was still blinded by the windshield ice. He was able to see an airliner ahead of him on the approach. When the tower turned the runway lights to the brightest level, the pilot saw the airport and selected Runway 15.

The tower provided wind checks for the Lance all the way down final, 180 at 22, 170 at 21 and 170 at 24. Just when it appeared that he had the situation well in hand, the pilot said, "I just experienced what I think to be windsh..." The last word was unintelligible.

The tower gave one more wind check, which was acknowledged by the pilot. The next words were those of the controller, "He just went in. He crashed at the approach end!"

So Close

A number of people witnessed the crash. The most graphic and accurate account was that of an airline co-pilot who saw the whole thing from his cockpit.

The co-pilot submitted the following statement during the investigation:

A set of navigation lights were observed on a two-mile final approach. When the aircraft was one mile out and about 500-600 feet agl, the lights and the aircraft abruptly pitched down with a sudden loss of about 100 feet.

This pitch down was followed by a sudden pitch up of about 100 to 150 feet, then another pitch down with a loss of altitude of about 300 feet, then a 300-foot pitch up followed by a very steep pitch down and the aircraft disappeared from view as it descended below the runway elevation and we both thought it had impacted short of Runway 15.

The aircraft reappeared in a near-vertical flight path and climbed rapidly to about 400-500 feet. As the aircraft pitched from the vertical up to the vertical down, a wing rocking of about 15 to 20 degrees about two cycles occurred. This pitch down, the steepest of the four, appeared nearly vertical from our vantage point and ended in an impact with the ground short of the threshold of Runway 15. A large fireball was observed, followed by a medium fire.

Wake Turbulence?

The sketch that accompanied the co-pilot's statement indicated that the Lance had entered a series of divergent pitch oscillations, each one larger in magnitude that the one before. Obviously, an out-of-control situation.

This led to speculation that N43J might have encountered the wake turbulence of the DC-9 that preceded it on the approach. Closer inspection of the times and distances involved, however, discounted this possibility.

Wind Shear?

Wind shear was also discussed and somewhat supported by the pilot's last words. Although a sudden change in wind speed and/or direction can certainly cause significant airspeed loss, it was considered unlikely with the amount of power available. The pilot should have been able to recover without the wild gyrations that he went through.

Normal Approach

It's highly likely that the pilot flew a normal approach, perhaps due to the fact that he was close to the runway after such a harrowing experience and didn't want to fly in a different configuration.

Normal procedures may have had a lot to do with this accident. When the airflow around an iced-up wing is suddenly and dramatically changed (as can happen when you lower the flaps), strange things can happen. The flaps were found fully extended, leading to a suspicion that the pilot opted for a completely normal approach and landing. He probably was surprised when the airplane became an unfamiliar and uncontrollable aerodynamic monster.

Even though the pilot said the ice was coming off, he couldn't see the tail. There may have been enough ice on the stabilator to cause a stall at approach speed. This could have resulted in a stall (pitch down), followed by a recovery and over-control (pitch up), with the cycle repeating and growing until impact.

No Guidance

There's not much in the books about flying an iced-up approach, especially in the handbooks of airplanes that aren't equipped for flight into icing. Since ice never forms in the same shape or amount, you become a test pilot in this situation.

Given all the unknowns, it's better to experiment at a safe altitude to find out about an airplane's low-speed behavior before committing to it close to the ground. It's better to land without flaps when there's ice on the airplane and at an airspeed that you know will provide adequate control.

Don't challenge icing conditions in an airplane that isn't equipped to do so. If you must go, be prepared to return to a non-icing environment at the first hint of ice. When you need a different altitude or heading to get out of ice, be assertive with ATC.

When you make a good decision to sit it out due to weather that's beyond the capabilities of the airplane, stay out until the weather improves. There's always some other less exciting way to get where you're going.